VOLUME 90 • NUMBER 4 • WINTER 2001

NATIONAL

CIVIC

REVIEW

MAKING CITIZEN DEMOCRACY WORK

IN THIS ISSUE

The American Communities Movement

T0340167

Christopher T. Gates
President, National Civic League

Robert Loper
Editor

A Publication of the National Civic League and Jossey-Bass

NATIONAL CIVIC REVIEW (ISSN 0027-9013) is published quarterly by Wiley Subscription Services, Inc., a Wiley company, at Jossey-Bass, 989 Market Street, San Francisco, CA 94103-1741, and the National Civic League, 1445 Market Street, Suite 300, Denver, CO 80202-1717. NCL, founded in 1894 as the National Municipal League, advocates a new civic agenda to create communities that work for everyone. NCL is a 501(c)(3) nonprofit, non-partisan educational association of individuals and organizations. NCL members have access to the information and services necessary to improve community life. For complete information, contact Derek Okubo, (303) 571-4343.

INDEXED in Public Affairs Information Service, ABC POL SCI, and Book Review Index.

SUBSCRIPTIONS are $55.00 per year for individuals and $105.00 per year for institutions. To order subscriptions, single issues, or reprints, please refer to the Ordering Information page at the back of this issue.

PERIODICALS postage paid at San Francisco, California, and at additional mailing offices. POSTMASTER: send address changes to National Civic Review, Jossey-Bass Inc., 989 Market Street, San Francisco, CA 94103-1741.

NCL MEMBERS send change of address to Debbie Gettings, National Civic League, 1445 Market Street, Suite 300, Denver, CO 80202-1717.

EDITORIAL CORRESPONDENCE should be sent to Robert Loper, National Civic League, 1319 F Street NW, Suite 204, Washington, DC, 20004.

www.josseybass.com

ISBN 978-0-7879-5821-3

LETTERS TO THE EDITOR. National Civic Review welcomes letters to the editor. Write to National Civic Review, 1319 F Street, Suite 204, Washington, DC, 20004, or send e-mail to robert@ncldc.org. Please include your name, address, and telephone number.

CONTENTS

NOTE FROM THE PRESIDENT

Events over the past year, from the election of 2000 to the tragedy of September 11, have changed how we think about and practice politics in this country. Easy assumptions of endless economic expansion amid ever-rising stock prices, ensured by an end to history, belong to another time. We have been forcibly reminded of the imprudence of complacency and the necessity of continuous engagement in a world where such hazards breed. We have learned again that politics, as it has always been, is a collective activity in which what is at stake extends to the most basic and ultimate of values and ends.

It has often been said that in light of September 11 everything is now different. In some sense this must be true, but we are still closer to the beginning than the end of what has begun. Whatever else has changed, each of us has been led to reassess the value we place on the things we regard as important. New circumstances change our sense of the relative importance of our various desires, objectives, and ends in comparison with one another.

This refocusing on the things that matter seems to have reconfirmed for many that, although they are not rescue workers and not in the military, what they do nevertheless makes an important contribution to the overall richness of our democratic society. There have been recurring anecdotes in the media about people from diverse vocations coming to this viewpoint after wrestling with their sense of how what they do matters in these times. People who are actively involved in community improvement efforts may not have previously experienced quite the same degree of concern about the value of their particular work. But the changed world we now inhabit and the new level of urgency conferred upon our politics should encourage us all to think more deeply about the kind of society we want to create and about how we can improve our efforts to do so.

In some small way, we hope that this issue of the *National Civic Review* makes a contribution to this process. Civic participation, community engagement, and collaborative decision making are all important values that guide the work of the National Civic League, as well as that of numerous other organizations concerned with reenergizing a dynamic and vibrant civil society and democratic polity. This issue of the *Review* recognizes some of the most interesting work being done by community movements and contains articles by leading practitioners on the promise heralded by convergence among these movements.

Community-level reform movements of all kinds have become a significant part of the political landscape across the United States. With the benefit of generous assistance from the W. K. Kellogg Foundation, the National Civic League and the Coalition for Healthier Cities and Communities convened a series of dialogues over the past year in six locations around the country. The purpose of this project was to assess the prospects for convergence among several of the community movements that have been most influential over the last decade. There are important differences among these groups, as is indicated by their descriptors: healthy communities, sustainable communities, livable communities, and so on. But there are areas of commonality as well that are the basis for sharing ideas and practices and that might lead to something that could be called a "communities movement."

The framing article by Kesler and O'Connor describes the communities project and gives some interesting detail about a new developmental stage, something they call the next stage of the civic sector. Community change work often requires both a neutral convener who can bring people together and a safe space for dialogue among participants. As the civic sector becomes more developed, this combination is being institutionalized in ways that enable communities to consolidate the advances they make and develop the capacity needed to sustain and extend their work.

Jacksonville Community Council Inc. (JCCI), in Florida, is one of the most well-established community organizations in the country; it is an excellent example of this next stage in the development of the civic sector. The article by David Swain, associate director of JCCI, takes an insightful look at the obstacles and opportunities encountered in a community improvement project and draws on JCCI's experience to illustrate these observations. An ongoing JCCI project deals with community indicators, which is a topic of widely shared concern across community movements.

The article by Randa Gahin and Chris Paterson presents a historical overview of community indicators work and assesses where the field is today. Finally, the article by Becky Miles-Polka details an innovative model being developed in Des Moines, Iowa, that takes an investment-based approach to human service delivery.

Taken together, the articles in this issue showcase the innovative activity of community movements and chart the path of future development. The public deliberation and civic participation that these movements engender are essential resources for our democratic republic. Governments at all levels—federal, state, and local—confront problems that they cannot resolve on their own even if there is political agreement to act upon them. Citizen engagement, through deliberation and action, can bring new ideas and capacities to bear. As politics is about shaping the society in which we live, an active citizenry can enlarge the scope of what is possible and help create a desirable world. The strength of community movements, acting independently and in concert with one another, is an encouraging sign of collective rededication to our enduring political ideals.

CHRISTOPHER T. GATES
PRESIDENT, NATIONAL CIVIC LEAGUE

The American Communities Movement

John T. Kesler, Drew O'Connor

Across the United States, a number of community-based movements and local groups share complementary visions and approaches to community transformation. This article gives an overview of these movements and examines some of their common concerns. In 2000, the National Civic League and the Coalition for Healthier Cities and Communities received a grant from the W. K. Kellogg Foundation to evaluate the potential for convergence of these community movements into a "communities movement." Although we found that it is too early to speak of the latter, a new stage in the development of community-based movements is emerging. The Communities Movement Project was designed as a series of five dialogues in locations around the country. The first stage was to convene an advisory council to frame the issues that would be discussed, choose the locations for the dialogues, and design a survey instrument for use in each dialogue. At the outset, we determined that we were interested in convening members of these community movements: Healthy Communities, Sustainable Communities, Community Building, Civic Democracy, Livable Communities, Safe Communities, and Smart Growth. There are other significant community-based movements, but this selection comprises a good sample of the movements that have been the most influential over the past decade. More information on each movement is found in this article.

The survey was designed to collect information from each organization on its main purpose, alignment with community-based movements, areas of emphasis, and underlying values. A copy of the survey is included as the Appendix to this article.

The survey asked respondents which, if any, of the seven movements their organization was most closely aligned with. (Respondents could also indicate another movement with which they identified, or report that their organization was not allied with any community-based movement.) Following that, respondents ranked their organization's five most important areas of emphasis from a list of twelve and ranked the importance of each of five values to their work.

The Dialogues

Daylong dialogues were held in Des Moines, Iowa; White River Junction, Vermont; Jacksonville, Florida; Salt Lake City, Utah; and Washington, D.C. For each dialogue except the one in Washington, we attempted to include "hidden leaders" in the community along with more easily identifiable members of established community movements. The Washington dialogue convened leaders of national movements to discuss the findings from the previous dialogues and to assess future directions. A standard format was followed for each of the other dialogues.

Early discussions among the convened group focused on the particular orientation of the participants and examined the degree to which they shared core values and principles. There was general agreement within all of the groups on the importance of a sense of community and the need to promote citizen involvement in decision making and develop leadership in the community. With this as a foundation, each dialogue focused on identifying locally shared priorities and the barriers that existed to pursuing their attainment. Next steps were discussed, and consideration was given to whether the participants might work together in the future. Each group was also asked about the potential its members saw for developing a communities movement. The outcome of each dialogue is summarized in the next section.

Des Moines, Iowa. The dialogue in Des Moines had the most local orientation, in that it included the fewest participants who identified with any of the nationally established community movements. Stakeholders from the public, private, and civic sectors were convened in a central-city neighborhood to focus on a few core issues of importance to the local community.

The primary topics were housing and children. One of those magical moments in this type of work happened during the course of this dialogue. After discussion within the group about shared community values, certain participants who had come to the meeting specifically to address other issues ended up forming a task force with the group to develop a community green space and resource area on a plot of vacant land. This subset of individuals, in concert with the others, transcended their particular interests to come together for a shared community purpose.

White River Junction, Vermont. The Vermont dialogue gave us our best opportunity to meet with professionals from the various community movements. The participants were from a four-state New England region, with many of them coming from New Hampshire and Vermont. The discussion about areas of common concern dealt with issues that were larger in scope than those of the other regional dialogues.

Much of the conversation centered on education and communication between community movements, social capital, systems and systems thinking, funding systems, and mechanisms of community-based projects. These issues may constitute a basis for convergence among the community movements. The meeting also spotlighted inherent barriers at the state and federal levels that impede development of cross-sector, cross-movement work at the community level. Categorical funding structures and lack of funder emphasis on social capital or civic issues were also cited as obstacles to achieving more integrated community-based work.

Jacksonville, Florida. The Jacksonville area has one of the strongest traditions of communitywide, multisectoral collaboration in the United States. Although the participants in this discussion showed some interest in process issues pertaining to community-based movements and projects, they focused more directly on two specific issues germane to the area: regionalism and education. Participants assessed resources and challenges and proposed sets of potential strategies. The clearest message that emerged from this meeting was that a compelling community issue can be an effective catalyst for producing synergy among community movements.

Salt Lake City, Utah. The county around Salt Lake City contains almost half the population of the state of Utah. There are a large number of community-based groups across the area, but little collaboration across jurisdictional lines. The Salt Lake City dialogue was an interesting contrast to the one in Jacksonville. Participants were drawn from the region around the city; most of them worked with nonprofits and government agencies broadly focused on improving the quality of life within local communities. Yet there were few significant examples of cross-sector endeavors among these groups, although there was great interest in moving in that direction. Understandably, this dialogue focused primarily on process issues related to collaborative community-based approaches.

The discussion did not move to concrete community issues as in Jacksonville. But the experience of being together and identifying similarities did create a lot of positive energy and plans for follow-up meetings.

Washington, D.C. Attendees of the Washington meeting were primarily locally based representatives of national organizations and agencies that concentrate on community-based activity and citizen involvement. We presented our preliminary evaluations of the prior dialogues to this group for discussion.

Two significant issues emerged. There is no evidence of an all-encompassing communities movement, and many questioned what the utility of such a structure would be. Most participants did agree, however, that there are a set of underlying values, tools, and goals that the community movements share and that integration among the movements could serve to maximize resources and enhance the impact of community transformation projects. The other issue concerned the importance of the civic sector in communities—that notional place where dialogue and deliberation occur, where trust is built, and where the foundation for community problem solving is developed. There was general agreement that a viable civic sector is essential for the work of each community movement. Enhancing the civic sector can increase the impact of community movements and their attendant projects and initiatives.

Observations on the Seven Movements

The survey results on identification with community movements were interesting. Some respondents indicated affiliation with each of the seven. Responses from affiliates of particular community-based movements showed considerable consistency across the community dialogues. But interesting nuances were evident that differed from general descriptions of the movements in the literature or input from the national leaders of those movements who were on the advisory council. The survey sample was too small to afford conclusive information, but the results are nonetheless suggestive. Here are brief summaries of some of the highlights.

The Healthy Community Movement. Respondents who identified most closely with the healthy community movement ranked physical health, mental health, and public health higher than the other movements and gave lower emphasis to developing a sense of community. This supports the observation that even though the healthy community movement attempts to model health in a broad sense, its roots in the traditional health sector are very much evident. Compared to respondents who most closely identified with the community building movement, those identifying with the healthy community movement placed more emphasis on human flourishing and less emphasis on justice. The community building movement has a similar process approach to community transformation. These differences in emphasis help confirm the impression that the healthy community movement tends to focus on issues of greater interest to the middle class and does not connect as deeply to justice-related themes that more directly affect other sectors of the community.

The Sustainable Community Movement. Respondents who self-identified with the sustainable community movement ranked human and natural ecologies and the interconnection of personal, community, and environmental flourishing as their most important areas of emphasis. They were the only ones to score concern for nonhuman life in the top five. The national leadership of this movement has voiced concern about perhaps needing to integrate notions pertaining to the quality of human life and community more fully within their conception of a sustainable community. However, in our survey the sustainable community respondents ranked the importance of a shared sense of community as their second highest category, as did respondents associated with two of the other movements.

The Community Building Movement. Respondents identifying with the community building movement ranked the importance of a sense of community higher than did any other group. They also gave a high ranking to safety, possibly reflecting the fact that the community building movement tends to concentrate on relatively impoverished socioeconomic areas, which may have a more pronounced concern with safety. The community building respondents rated justice as their highest value, as did the civic democracy and safe community respondents. The community building movement respondents gave a higher ranking to spiritual concerns than any other movement, with healthy community respondents being a distant second.

The Livable Community Movement. Survey responses by individuals identifying with the livable community movement reflected the architect and city planner orientation of this movement. They ranked the built environment and economic growth and development as their most important areas of emphasis. Yet livable community respondents also ranked the importance of civility and civil discourse as third in importance, higher than any other group for this variable.

The Civic Democracy Movement. The civic democracy movement understandably ranked political and democratic processes as their most important area of emphasis, followed by organizational infrastructure. This movement is deeply committed to institutional and process aspects of community functioning, and it recognizes the importance of a shared purpose of community. Civic democracy respondents strongly emphasized the importance of basic survival and sustainability; social justice; and higher levels of human, community, and environmental flourishing, demonstrating a broad spectrum of concern grounded in basic themes of survival and justice.

The Safe Community Movement. The safe community movement is probably less well organized at the national level than most of the other community movements. Survey results indicated that respondents identifying with this movement viewed safety and physical health as their highest concerns. They also ranked basic sustainability and social justice along with higher levels of human, community, and environmental flourishing as their most important underlying values.

The Smart Growth Movement. Respondents identifying with the smart growth movement were most concerned with economic development, organizational infrastructure, the built environment, and political infrastructure. Along with adherents from the sustainable and livable community movements, smart growth movement respondents ranked environmental concerns highly. There are many similarities between the smart growth and the livable community movements, as both share emphasis on environmental sustainability and economic development.

Common Themes Among the Community Movements

By using surveys and facilitating dialogues, we were able to get a detailed sense of the concerns of community movement participants in different parts of the country. As a prelude to assessing the potential for convergence among these movements, it is essential that we have a clear understanding of the values and areas of emphasis that underlie and orient these community movements. Our observations on the content and process themes that define these movements are presented here.

Content Themes. It should come as no surprise that a shared *sense of community* was the most frequently cited area of emphasis among the community-based movements. This category was ranked in the top three by representatives of all of the movements except the livable community and smart growth groups. All of the dialogues that we convened confirm the importance of this focal point. Similarly, the emphasis given to the civic sector in the Washington meeting complements this community orientation.

We asked people in the dialogues about their *sense of the natural environment* and feelings about the interconnection of personal, community, and environmental flourishing. There was general acknowledgment of the importance of ecological sensitivity, but no group other than the sustainability group ranked human and natural ecologies in its top four categories of importance. Livable community and smart growth respondents listed the category as fifth in their order of concerns. Representatives of the sustainability movement on the advisory council said they viewed the environment as being interconnected with human ecology and spirituality. Interestingly, sustainability movement representatives in the community dialogues ranked the importance of a sense of community higher than the healthy community people did.

Social justice is at least an implicit theme in all of the community-based movements. Ensuring that the full diversity of the community is included in deliberation, collaboration, and decision making is a shared concern of all of these movements. The community building movement has perhaps the strongest social justice orientation, as it primarily targets the needs and interests of residents in lower-income urban areas. The sustainability movement was the only group to rank a concern for nonhuman life in its top ten concerns, ranking it fifth. Theirs was the only group to rank environmental justice highly. For the handful of attendees at the dialogues who indicated that they identified with movements other than those listed, nonhuman life was their highest concern; they ranked environmental justice, a shared sense of community, and social justice themes highly as well.

The final content theme is *process as substance.* On the whole, these groups are committed to the process of community building in terms of supporting ongoing dialogue, implementing continuous feedback loops, and practicing inclusive collaboration and decision making. In this sense, there is widespread awareness of the importance of civic infrastructure and the civic health of the community. Given the centrality of these issues to the civic democracy movement, this movement could play a vital role in developing a broader communities movement.

Operational and Process Themes. The first operational and process theme is *inclusive, ongoing, value-based dialogue.* From a process perspective, the ideal approach for most community-based groups is to include all stakeholders in a deliberative process conducted in terms of shared vision and values rather than on the basis of power or interests. This approach is intended to elicit a sense of the common good. The importance given to deliberative democracy in the community dialogues underscores this preference. Some groups, such as the sustainability movement, may sometimes put more emphasis on pursuing a principled agenda than on modeling inclusive collaboration and dialogue in the community. Others, such as the civic democracy and healthy community movements, see inclusive community collaboration and dialogue as fundamental to everything they do.

Experienced practitioners among the participants in the dialogues well understand the need to use *indicators* in their work to get their initiatives funded. Measurement tools such as indicators are needed to assess progress and to lay the foundation for consistent and intelligent policy design. Creation of community-based, community-owned indicators can be an important means of empowering citizens through giving them information about conditions that affect their lives. The process of designing community-based indicators can also increase citizen participation in developing public policy.

Participants agreed on the importance of laying the groundwork for *public policy* development. As community decision making moves beyond particular concerns and interest-based activism, there is growing recognition of the need to enhance the civic sector within communities. An increased level of citizen involvement is needed to shape the broader community agenda. In some areas, particularly Jacksonville, structures, tools, and processes are in place to facilitate such involvement.

Community-based groups all need a basic level of *organizational competency* to pursue the goals for which they were created. To maintain themselves and expand their impact, this basic level must be enhanced. Among the most important competencies required are fundraising and sustainability strategies, a capacity to be inclusive and engage major stakeholders, the ability to develop goals and strategies for the long run, and the determination to overcome political and bureaucratic barriers.

Is There a Communities Movement? Could There Be?

This project began out of an interest in assessing the prospects for building a communities movement. We have determined that there are a large number of common and complementary substantive and operational themes among community-based movements. In all of our dialogues, participants were struck by their interconnection, the number of shared or similar values and priorities, and the common interest in broader community transformation. By contrast, there was not much evidence of collaboration among the various community-based movements.

On the neighborhood level, the people in Des Moines had little awareness of the presence of these movements in their own community, yet almost all of them saw that their own priorities were closely aligned with those of at least one of the major movements. In Jacksonville, however, there is such a strong collaborative tradition that it was really a matter of common sense for everyone to be drawn together in convening and collaborating capacities.

The most sophisticated and experienced group of practitioners participating in this project were those gathered in White River Junction. Yet they did not have much experience in linking and collaborating with other movements, and because of their wide dispersal over a multistate region they did not think there was much potential for collaborative follow-up among the dialogue participants. In Salt Lake City, it was uniformly expressed that there has been increasingly more communication and collaboration among community-based groups in the Salt Lake Valley over the last ten years. However, collaboration and activity across jurisdictional lines was the exception rather than the rule. In sum, we would have to conclude that there is not even what one might loosely call a communities movement.

Still, there is no question that the substantive and operational themes of the major community-based movements are similar or complementary. All these movements share an interest in community transformation. Although the environmental and sustainability theme is not a core part of most of these movements, our conversations in the dialogues reflected general appreciation for the importance of both human and environmental sustainability. Clearly, themes such as a sense of community, social justice, process as substance, indicator development, and public policy formation are areas of mutual interest among the movements and could be the basis for some degree of convergence.

There was not much interest among the various movements in merging their agendas and identities. Nonetheless, an enormous amount of untapped potential exists for the various community-based movements to learn from one another and collaborate. No one, including the advisory council members and the participants in the Washington meeting, was aware of any convening force for bringing distinct but complementary groups together for broader collaboration, on a regional or national level. Yet there was virtually unanimous enthusiasm for an integrative communities movement, that is, one that links existing groups in complementary ways to achieve more fundamental community transformation and promote greater awareness of the interconnections among personal, community, and environmental well being.

Next Steps for a Communities Movement

It is unclear whether an authentic communities movement will be produced by the convergence among movements. But steps can be taken to promote an integrative vision and develop the institutional capacity for greater collaborative efforts.

Integrative Vision. Although there may be a motivation for some groups or movements to merge into something more encompassing, most of the community-based movements seem deeply invested in their particular agenda. But if the emphasis is on integration rather than merger, each group can maintain its identity while collaborating with others. This approach may require a different conception of what a communities movement could be—something that has more of a spontaneous, organic, and fluid character than something that is marked by organizational rigidity. The points of convergence raised in this article may offer a basis for conversation among the national leadership of the main community movements to pursue more specific strategies for integration.

The Next Stage of the Civic Sector. Throughout this article, reference has been made to the critical importance of the civic sector for all of the community-based movements. In traditional terms, we think of the civic sector as comprising those places where people connect and become involved, through a variety of activities, in their neighborhood, church, association, and other organizations. The civic sector nurtures issue-based activism around areas such as health care, education, housing, economic development, and environmental protection.

Over the course of this project, we have come to realize that something new is beginning to emerge in communities across the United States. We call this the next stage of the civic sector, and it is the product of the community movements themselves. More sophisticated organizational capacities are emerging from the smaller civic forums and informal civic practices and habits that exist in communities. This development generates enhanced information and more stable processes and structures; perhaps most important, it also creates a neutral space for deliberation on critical community issues. The next stage of the civic sector is informed by the values and tools of the community movements, such as the deliberative practices of civic democracy, indicator development from the sustainability movement, equity from community builders, and the visioning and convening tools of the healthy community movement.

Jacksonville Community Council Incorporated (JCCI) is perhaps the best illustration of this next stage. JCCI is a 501(c)(3) established in 1975 through support of the chamber of commerce. Over the years, it has developed the capacity to convene citizens across sectors, inform them with relevant indicators and data, and engage them in studying critical community issues and developing action plans to improve the overall quality of life in Jacksonville. JCCI has figured out how to give civic participation an impact on public policy and has provided an ongoing structure to do so. (The article by David Swain in this issue is a detailed account of JCCI and its history and activities.) Other organizations such as the Boulder, Colorado, County Civic Forum, which evolved from a healthy communities initiative; Innovation Partnerships of Portland, Oregon, a 501(c)(3) that was catalyzed by the mayor and local business leaders; and Vision 2020 of Greater Lafayette, Indiana, a newly formed entity that has evolved from a community visioning and strategic planning project, have separately and organically developed similar sets of capacities and roles in varying degrees with individual nuances.

From what we've seen so far, organizations that constitute the next stage of the civic sector will create neutral spaces for public deliberation, produce good information on community issues, lead planning activities that result in action, and amplify citizen voices at the public policy level. We will continue to study this phenomenon to determine how and why it emerges, what its level of impact is, and whether it can be catalyzed and replicated in other settings. Future articles in this journal will develop theoretical and conceptual analyses of this next stage of the civic sector.

In several of our community movement discussions, we heard that nationally based movements don't really matter at the local level. People care about issues and not movements. It is possible that the next stage of the civic sector will combine the values and tools of national movements with the energy of citizens engaged with the critical issues affecting their communities to create a dynamic entity that fulfills a new and much needed role in today's society.

Appendix: Questionnaire for Regional Meeting

Main Purpose of Your Organization
On the back of this sheet, in just a few sentences write the name, location, and main mission and types of activity of the community-based organization which you represent. If you are involved with several organizations, describe the one with which you most closely identify and answer below accordingly.

Community-Based Movement Alignment
Check the community-based movement with which your organization is most closely aligned or identifies:

❑ Healthy communities
❑ Community building
❑ Sustainable communities (natural environmental emphasis)
❑ Livable communities (emphasis on built environment)
❑ Civic democracy
❑ Safe communities
❑ Economic development and growth
❑ No connection or identification with any community-based movement
❑ Other community-based movement (designate):_____

The following areas and levels are not comprehensive and the rankings are not precise, but your filling out the following will help provide a general sense of how various community based organizations and movements that will be represented at this and other regional meetings compare to one another with regard to selected indicators.

Areas of Emphasis of Your Organization

Check the areas of emphasis that are explicitly important to your organization and then rank in order the top five areas that you have checked, with 1 being the highest.

Check   Rank

☐   _____   Physical health
☐   _____   Safety
☐   _____   Mental and psychological well-being
☐   _____   Healthy organizational infrastructure in the community (civil society)
☐   _____   Shared sense of community and purpose
☐   _____   Healthy political and democratic processes
☐   _____   Civility and civil discourse
☐   _____   Healthy economic development and growth
☐   _____   Flourishing nonhuman life
☐   _____   Flourishing human and natural ecologies
☐   _____   Well-designed man-made environments
☐   _____   Interconnected individual, community, and environmental flourishing

Underlying Values of Your Organization

Rank from 1 to 4, with 1 being most important, the values of your organization:

Rank

_____   Basic sustainability for future generations
_____   Equity and social justice
_____   Higher levels of human, community, and environmental prosperity
_____   Spiritual concerns
_____   Other:_____

John T. Kesler is executive director of the U.S. Coalition for Healthier Cities and Communities.

Drew O'Connor is the director of community services in the Denver office of the National Civic League.

Civic Gemstones: The Emergent Communities Movement

Tyler Norris

> What we seek—at every level—is pluralism that achieves some kind of coherence, wholeness incorporating diversity. Diversity is not simply "good" in that it implies a breadth of tolerance and sympathy. A community of diverse elements has greater capacity to adapt and renew itself in a swiftly changing world.
>
> —John Gardner, *Building Community* (1991)

The fire and brilliance of a beautiful gemstone derives from the angular arrangement of its many facets reflecting upon each other. Similarly, the vibrancy of civic life in America emerges from the interaction of its many diverse facets. Today, these facets are unique citizen movements, taking sustained action toward measurably improving human well-being and community quality of life.

Known by scores of names (among which Healthy Communities, Sustainable Communities, Livable Communities, Safe Communities, Whole Communities, and Smart Growth are probably the most well known), these citizen movements are locally driven, deeply inclusive change efforts constituting a phenomenon that can be described as a communities movement.

These collaborative, participatory, multisectoral initiatives are multiplying and thriving, addressing an array of pressing issues facing society. Seen synergistically, they are a natural evolution of democracy's promise and define a greater movement that is only now coming into focus and prominence.

The communities movement is a working model of what John Gardner calls "a community of diverse elements." As such, it has the potential to deliver on what Dr. Len Duhl and Dr. Trevor Hancock called for early in the Healthy Cities, Healthy Communities movement, that is, to be "continually creating and improving those physical and social environments, and expanding those community resources which enable people to mutually support each other in performing all the functions of life and in developing to their maximum potential"[1] (see the Appendix to this article).

The Roots of a Movement

Alexis de Tocqueville's *Democracy in America* remains a touchstone for thinking about the American penchant for self-governance.[2] De Tocqueville wrote of deliberation and decision making at every level by common people. He highlighted self-determined groups framing issues, offering solutions, and organizing themselves to carry out desired change. He chronicled the existence of inclusive and conducive social spaces, forming the center of authentic community and performing its most vital functions.

One hundred seventy years after de Tocqueville's keen observations, American civic life remains populated with associations of community members engaged with the tasks of local governance. Although much of this activity may be poorly understood by policy makers, and trivialized or ignored by the media, it has the power to revitalize our democracy at every level. Citizen or participatory democracy may operate below the radar screen of most pundits, but its structures and processes help to define the social space within which leaders engage diverse stakeholders to address the issues of the day.

A Collaborative Explosion

Since the early 1960s in the United States, literally thousands of public-private partnerships have been formed to work for economic development, educational improvement, environmental protection, health care, social issues, better land use, and other core issues. The best of these partnerships bring the usual suspects together with those not traditionally seated at the decision-making table. These initiatives are engaging a new wave of voluntarism across sectors, generations, perspectives, and cultures. An array of groups, including chambers of commerce, United Ways, governmental agencies, hospitals, community colleges, health departments, neighborhood and community-based organizations, and places of worship, convene these new partnerships. Even more important than who they are is how they practice what civic educator Gruffie Clough calls *facilitative leadership*.[3]

The most successful of these partnerships cross boundaries and work across lines that were only rarely transcended in previous eras.[4] Some of them are formed by citizen leaders or social entrepreneurs, who, regardless of background (grassroots, nonprofit, or corporate) and with varying resources behind them, bring a new emphasis on risk taking, outcomes orientation, and sustainability into the civic sphere.

Some of these alliances are narrow in theme but tackle a specific problem or set of interrelated complex issues; others are broader in scope. Some are, at their core, convening entities, attempting to address the root of civic decline that Peter Drucker speaks of in *Leading Beyond the Walls*: "All earlier pluralistic societies destroyed themselves, because no one took care of the common good. They [civic groups] abounded in communities, but could not sustain community, let alone create it."[5] New civic convening entities—such as the Citizens League of Central Oklahoma, founded in 1992—play a catalytic role on behalf of the greater community, whether framing issues in forums for public deliberation or hosting long-term planning processes that serve to create a sense of direction, shared leadership, and resource alignment around top priorities.

This expansion of community-based organizations and multisector partnerships has led to renewed civic vitality and generated tangible positive outcomes. Much of the improvement in public health, community revitalization, and quality of life in recent decades can be attributed to these alliances.[6] Although a number of these nascent organizations have floundered, participants in these movements recognize that failure is part of learning by doing and can generate conditions for improving the next round of program design. This mature leadership mind-set is part of the foundation for continuous development of citizen democracy.

Seeing Yourself in the Other's Reflection

In the United States today, well over thirty thousand citizens' groups, nongovernmental organizations, civic partnerships, and foundations are addressing the myriad issues of health and quality of life—economic, ecological, human, and social sustainability in the broadest sense. Globally, the number is greater than one hundred thousand.

Businessman and *Natural Capitalism* coauthor Paul Hawken recently took a "thirty-thousand-foot view" of this activity for the *Utne Reader*: "If you ask these groups for their principles, frameworks, conventions, models or declarations, you will find that they do not conflict. Never before in history has this happened. In the past, movements that became powerful started with a unified or centralized set of ideas (Marxism, Christianity, Freudianism) and then disseminated them . . . [but the community-level movements] did not start this way."[7] Len Duhl describes the movement as spontaneously self-organizing.

Hawken and others note that though this movement is not marked by wholesale concurrence on top priorities and specific strategies (which probably should not exist in a dynamic democratic process), there is widespread agreement on fundamental values. This shared outlook is likely to be due in some measure to the number of "cultural creatives" who are active in these various movements. The term is used by sociologist Paul Ray (and others) to describe the estimated 25 percent of the U.S. adult population who share a value orientation prizing civil rights, the environment, jobs and social justice, gay and lesbian rights, alternative health care, and personal growth, among other goals, and who are deeply suspicious of the effects of globalization on local community.[8]

But cultural creatives are not the only ones involved in these organizations. Indeed, the leadership of this movement is drawn from all sectors of society and all parts of town. The communities movement is the modern face of de Tocqueville's view of our democracy, with its leadership arising from every culture, ethnicity, race, faith, and preference to bring together people with very different economic, education, and social experiences to do the work that must be done for the commons. This approach requires a whole-systems mind-set. It is sparked by the kind of realization triggered by the first photograph of the earth from space. We live in one socioecosystem; there is no "away." What affects one person, on what Buckminster Fuller called "Spaceship Earth," affects us all. These systems-thinking leaders are bringing their core values and beliefs into alignment with the way they want to live and are developing social innovations that can transform what ails us.

The movement grows as a spontaneous, natural expression of people in communities rising to the occasion of dealing with the issues they encounter in daily life. No one is in charge, there are few limits, and no one is holding anyone back. There are national and global organizations spurring their development, and large networks forming rapidly via the Web, but at the core it remains a locally driven phenomenon. This is a vital and evolving way of doing the public's business. No one claims to have all the answers. There is no one model; the best organizations are highly nimble and flexible, not surprisingly mirroring the dynamics of the most profitable business enterprises.

Emergent Patterns

Some years ago, Trevor Hancock (an early inspirator of the healthy cities movement) and I compared notes on the dozens of community visions we had helped to generate. We were struck by how remarkably similar they were across neighborhoods, cities, cultures, and even nations. Generally, people aspire to very much the same things: from a dynamic local economy, a healthy ecosystem, and a vibrant downtown and social system to even the specifics of what a compelling neighborhood should contain.

Community analysis and a nationwide series of local dialogues conducted by the U.S. Coalition for Healthier Cities and Communities identified a shared ecological approach to problem solving among the communities studied. Each community had an evident commitment to shaping its own future and practiced collaborative resource sharing methodologies as a means of getting there. There was a common desire to build and engage leadership capacity among individuals from all corners of society. Techniques such as inclusive dialogue and broad-based engagement were used to create an enriched sense of community, and there was prominent use of indicators to measure progress and the impact of investments.[9]

Community activists should examine these patterns of successful practices and apply them creatively in their own local context. If there is one major lesson, it is that successful change starts with human relationships. Success requires more than just having the financial resources or structures, though they are important. The fundamental elements are the norms of trust and reciprocity and the networks of civic engagement that Robert Putnam has recently popularized in his work *Bowling Alone* as social capital. It takes a lot of work and meeting a lot of commitments to build authentic social capital, starting with the same common man and woman about which de Tocqueville spoke. This is democracy in action.

Design Principles

Many of the most effective community-based, multisectoral change initiatives making up the communities movement share a series of characteristics. The characteristics or principles listed here have been identified on the basis of experience with participatory learning in more than four hundred change efforts that addressed an array of human, social, ecological, health, economic, and quality-of-life issues.[10] They can be used as design principles or promising practices to guide future efforts. The community movements that are able to create and sustain positive outcomes tend to do certain things:

- *Use a broad definition of community.* A community can be defined by factors such as interest, sector, and profession as well as be determined by geographic area. Some of the most promising definitions pair community of place, such as a neighborhood or region, with community of interest, such as youth assets and workforce development.
- *Create a compelling vision from shared* values. A community's vision is the story of its desired future. To be powerful and inspiring, the vision should reflect the core values of its diverse members. A vision is not bullet points on a chart; it is a living expression of shared accountability to priorities. In the words of Suzanne Morse, of the Pew Partnership for Civic Change, "a community vision must include the ability to deliver a tangible product that is needed, usable and creates new value."[11]
- *Embrace a broad definition of health and well-being.* Health is more than the absence of disease. It is an optimum state of well-being—physical, mental, emotional, and spiritual. Health can be broadly defined to include a full range of quality-of-life issues. This definition recognizes that most of what creates health is related to lifestyle and behavior. Other major factors are genetic endowment and the socioeconomic, cultural, and physical environments. Thus, health is a by-product of an array of choices and factors, not simply the result of medical care intervention. One aspect, civic health, embraces the skills, processes, and relationships that form what Chris Gates of the National Civic League calls civic infrastructure. These elements constitute essentially the capacity to get good work done.[12]
- *Address quality of life for everyone.* Healthy and Sustainable Communities strive to ensure that the basic emotional, physical, and spiritual needs of

everyone in the community are attended to. Equity is a foundation of vital democratic process.

• *Engage diverse citizen participation and widespread community owner-ship.* In Healthy and Sustainable Communities, all people take active and ongoing responsibility for themselves, their families, their property, and their community. A leader's work is to find common ground among participants so that everyone is empowered to take direct action for their well-being and can influence community direction.

• *Focus on systems change.* No single organization or sector can offer full solutions to today's most vexing problems. A focus on systems change encom-passes how people live and work together. It involves how community services are delivered, how information is shared, how local governments operate, and how business is conducted. Systems change concerns resource allocation and decision making, not just doing nice projects. Addressing complex topics ranging from a healthy future for youth and urban sprawl to growing a dynamic local economy requires leaders from multiple sectors, each bringing creativity and resources to the table.

• *Build capacity using local assets and resources.* By developing an infra-structure that encourages and invests in the natural gifts, talents, and aspira-tions of people and their formal and informal associations, fewer resources need to be spent on back-end services that attempt to fix problems result-ing from a weak community infrastructure.[13] Accomplishing this requires starting from existing community strengths and successes and then investing in enhancement of a community's civic infrastructure.

• *Benchmark and measure progress and outcomes.* Communities committed to quality improvement over time use performance measures and community indicators to help expand the flow of information and accountability to all cit-izens. This information also reveals whether residents are heading toward or away from their stated goals. Timely, accurate information, translated into tan-gible action, is vital to sustaining long-term community improvement.

A Fresh Look at Movements

Healthy Communities help unleash human potential. They are the foundation for trust and relationships; they bestow a sense of place, identity, and belong-ing. They mobilize creativity and resources toward a shared vision for the future. Healthy communities both call for and nurture inspired leadership. They seek and reward diverse voices and sustained action for the common good.[14]

Successful change comes from working within and outside of established systems to bring about desired results. Often initiated by protest and aspira-tion for what is possible, movements for change have first challenged and then later defined the civic landscape. They have driven new behaviors, practices, and policies.

As important as individual courage and inspirational leadership are, the deeper force for sustained change goes beyond the efforts of individuals working alone. Consider the movements for human rights; suffrage; civil rights; peace; health and reproductive rights; environmental protection; community renewal; and most recently biogenetic, economic, cultural, and ecological sustainability in a world marketplace. These movements have fostered and grown, and have had an impact on, the context of millions of choices made daily by individuals in communities of interest and place. Ordinary people cultivate cultures within which behaviors and practices are both reinvented and reinforced in homes, neighborhoods, businesses, places of worship, and the policy arena.

We need to be mindful of this perspective as we address the myriad issues confronting our lives today. On virtually every front, there is much work to be done. We need to improve the quality of our education system, create vibrant local economies, promote ethical leadership behavior, ensure that jobs pay livable wages for families, sustain a healthy environment, and ensure access to adequate and affordable housing and primary care and preventive services. Among the numerous goals and values we seek to advance are development of dynamic and mutually respectful faith communities; effective and responsive governance; strong families and support networks; widespread opportunities for recreation and artistic expression; active lifelong voluntarism; and livable, walkable, safe neighborhoods that promote land use while minimizing sprawl and preserving a sense of place.

A Call for Convergence

Common Cause founder and former National Civic League Chairman John Gardner has spoken of the need to grow networks of responsibility in all parts of a community. This differs significantly from the blue-ribbon panel methodology of gathering the anointed, or seeking the ephemeral white knight, or hiring the hottest consultant with the new magic bullet. It requires connecting the diverse and essential parts of a community with a shared vision and aspirations, and then collaboratively growing the capacity and sense of responsibility to take action. This is an issue of leadership for the whole community, not just for those in traditional positions of power.

Given the many facets—indeed assets—of the communities movement, one challenge for the early twenty-first century is to produce convergence among them. It is time for a deliberate focus on shared learning, alignment of networks and resources, and a galvanized leadership agenda across the individual movements. We must create a synergy that draws on the core competencies and objectives of each and that can accelerate the personal, organizational, and public policy change sought by all.

Each facet of the communities movement has its favorite issues and founding sector (health care, environmental organizations, land use planners, social service agencies, interfaith groups, economic developers, downtown promoters, and so on). Although each is a necessary part of the solution, none is sufficient by itself to create the changes to which all aspire. We cannot fix schools and improve educational outcomes by addressing just teachers. Nor can we improve health outcomes simply by fixing hospitals, or reduce crime by reorienting police. The recent lessons demonstrated by the well-intentioned (but mostly ineffective) DARE program to stop drug use in schools makes this point brilliantly. Each diverse facet of the communities movement must be integrated into a shared effort to address all of the issues.

John Kesler, executive director of the U.S. Coalition for Healthier Cities and Communities, puts it this way: "The communities movement entails an effort to link the various community-based movements while maintaining the integrity of each in order to further benefit communities by building on what these movements have in common and highlighting their unique and valuable differences. There is an emphasis then on integration not merger, on collaboration and synergy toward the common goal of community transformation."[15]

Perhaps an essential community leadership function is to seek greater discipline in pursuing this synergy from disparate, and valuable, local assets. Today, America's civic landscape is one of intense cooperation and fragmentation, where there is much talk but little collaboration among the collaboratives. For example, if the Healthy Community people aren't working with the Livable Community people, we will keep building cities and transportation approaches that unwittingly promote sedentary lifestyles and cardiovascular disease. Shouldn't we encourage developers, architects, and transportation planners to contribute to health just as we do doctors and nurses?

Multifaceted, integrated approaches such as the ones listed here must become a norm rather than being an exception:

- *Community-supported agriculture:* produces great organic produce to urban areas while sustaining rural lands and a pastoral way of life
- *Microcredit:* makes very small loans to aspiring entrepreneurs, strengthening neighborhoods and increasing income
- *Transit-oriented development:* builds new housing developments and rehabilitates old neighborhoods next to transit links; doing so cuts pollution, saves commute time, and creates vibrant mixed-use neighborhoods
- *Sector-specific, communitywide workforce development strategies:* creates partnerships between specific employers and workers, such as health care providers and hard-to-place individuals, to match workforce needs with pools of people seeking employment
- *Voluntary simplicity:* minimizes unnecessary consumption and energy and materials waste, while attacking the source of work-life stressors driving physical, mental, emotional, spiritual, and family-life disease

There are a number of signs of progress. Led by business, government, and philanthropic leaders, collaborative funding practices and participatory governance structures are now becoming more common than their single-sector-approach predecessors. United Ways and community foundations nationwide are promoting new ways of investing in, and tracking return on investment from, initiatives they support. To take just one example, in the city of Boise, Idaho, young people are now in voting roles on every board and commission, no longer having just token participation on the parks and recreation committee.

New Measures for Health and Wealth

Development of community indicators and quality-of-life report cards holds serious promise for accelerating positive change.[16] Communities are looking for fresh approaches and promising ways to track their performance. Rather than simply gathering secondary data from institutions that measure only certain variables (financial, disease states, and so on) and not outcomes, it is time to redefine our concepts and develop ways to measure authentic community wealth. We will have better information concerning those issues we are most interested in, and these tools will also enable us to hold our leaders (and ourselves) accountable for realizing desired outcomes.

The concept of whole wealth encompasses a range of forms of capital: natural, economic, human, and social. Redefined in this way, wealth can be seen as an expression of a different form of capitalism, one that values resources by more than just economic criteria. A community-oriented capitalist would pursue transactions, practices, and policies that favor returns to all forms of capital.

A new investment strategy informed by this thinking is essential for ensuring sustainable progress by institutions as well as by communities and nations. It also opens new opportunities for innovation in products and services. In the future, these developments will help diverse groups and initiatives move beyond an all-too-common focus on narrow, quick-fix projects and solutions.

In Colorado, a program called Denver Benchmarks (supported and led by public, private, and nonprofit entities working together with neighborhood residents) will soon allow anyone with a modem, a computer, and an interest in improving the community to type in an address and get neighborhood-level social, health, economic, and other quality-of-life data. Individuals will be able to compare their neighborhood data with those of other neighborhoods, or with those of their city, county, or metro region. Easy access to a database of targeted, evidence-based, best practices will disseminate information about producing positive change. The system will then keep track of interventions and build a real-time local and national database of what works.

Innovations of this kind benefit everyone from policy makers to grassroots organizers (who can then in turn be empowered as citizen policy makers).

Imagine a middle school teacher using such a system for social studies classes—and then linking it to service learning projects in the community!

Making It Happen

At the heart of community change is how each of us rises to the occasion of being a member of the community in which we live, work, play, and worship. Our actions either build relationships, connections, and wholeness or they do not. There are no easy answers; instead, we must rely on our creativity, our best intentions, and each other. We must discover what our shared values are and then act upon them to build a healthier community.

Let us therefore weave together the multiple strands and unique genius of the communities movement. Let us make whole the civic gemstone, and heal the gulf between the conversations we have around our kitchen tables and the formal processes of governance, policy making, and resource allocation from which many feel so removed. Let us connect the wisdom and capacity of our neighborhoods with the thinking and strategies emerging from Washington. Let us gather the disparate and untapped human and social resources around us and generate the next chapter of the American story for a future de Tocqueville. Above all, let us make this story complete with tangible community outcomes worthy of the democracy with which we are entrusted:

> We will ever strive for the ideals and sacred things of the city,
> . . . both alone and with many
> We will unceasingly seek to quicken the sense of public duty
> We will revere and obey the city's laws
> We will transmit this city not only no less
> But greater, and more beautiful than it was transmitted to us
>
> —*Athenian Oath*

Appendix: Facets of the Communities Movement

Healthy Cities, Healthy Communities. This movement is based on a broad concept of health that conceives of personal, community, and environmental flourishing as being organically interconnected. It encourages collaborative, inclusive, and consensus-oriented community dialogue for community visioning and goal setting. The movement emphasizes both indicator-based community metrics as well as the art of community building. Initially spurred by the ideas of Dr. Len Duhl and Dr. Trevor Hancock, this approach was first implemented in Europe by the World Health Organization in the mid-1980s. In the United States, the National Civic League and a range of hospital and public health organizations helped spread the movement to more than twelve hundred cities. (www.healthycommunities.org)

Sustainable Communities. This movement works to produce communities that are environmentally sound, economically prosperous, and socially equitable. It emphasizes the importance of environmental protection and the interrelatedness of human and ecological stability. (www.sustainability.org)

Livable Communities. This approach assists communities in growing so as to ensure a high quality of life and strong, sustainable economic growth. It emphasizes the integrity and compatibility of the built environment with human and ecological well-being. (www.livable.com)

Safe Communities. Through a focus on occupational, community, and lifestyle issues, this movement promotes a culture of safety and well-being. There is particular emphasis on prevention of accidents and violence. (www.ncpc.org/2safer.htm)

Smart Growth. This initiative highlights the connections between development and quality of life. It leverages new growth to improve communities. Smart Growth initiatives invest time, attention, and resources in restoring community vitality to central cities and older suburbs. As communities continue to grow, this movement provides a scaffold to ensure that growth is well managed and beneficial for all. (www.smartgrowth.org)

Whole Communities. This movement is centered on the role of faith-based organizations in addressing a broad range of physical, mental, emotional, and spiritual health issues and values, including social justice, personal responsibility, and moral integrity. The movement is directed toward whole-person, whole-community health and is made operational by networks of transformative relationships within and across health and faith systems. (http://www.ihpnet.org)

Healthy Communities, Healthy Youth. This movement is active in more than six hundred communities in America and promotes long-term organizational and cultural change that supports healthy development for all children and adolescents. This work is grounded in the asset-based human development approach of the Search Institute. (www.search-institute.org)

100 Percent Access, Zero Health Disparities. The goal of this initiative is to ensure 100 percent access to health, with zero disparities, for each person in every community across America. More than five hundred communities are now working in locally defined ways toward this goal. (Tel. 813/221–9072; http://www.healthycommunities.org/cgi-bin/?MIval=faq)

Natural Capitalism. Groups like the Natural Step use a science- and systems-based approach to organizational planning for sustainability. They offer a practical set of design criteria that can be used to direct social, environmental, and economic actions. The Natural Step framework is based on integrated assessment of current economic, social, and ecological dynamics and the implications of present trends for human society. (www.naturalstep.org)

This list was in part adapted with permission from the Website of the U.S. Coalition for Healthier Cities and Communities (http://www.healthy-communities.org/healthycommunities.html).

Notes

1. Duhl, L., and Hancock, T. "Promoting Health in the Urban Context." (WHO Healthy Cities Papers.) Copenhagen, FADL, 1988, p. 4.

2. De Tocqueville, A. *Democracy in America.* New York: New American Library, 1956. (Originally published in 1835)

3. Ayre, D., Clough, G., and Norris, T. *Facilitating Community Change.* San Francisco: Grove, 2000, pp. 2–36. Facilitative leadership is that collection of tools, techniques, and behaviors that help the group, and individuals within the group operate at the highest levels of efficiency, effectiveness, and productivity, while increasing the self-confidence of all involved.

4. Peirce, N., and Johnson, C. *Boundary Crossers: Community Leadership for a Global Age.* College Park, Md.: James McGregor Burns Academy of Leadership, 1997, p. 9.

5. Drucker, P. "The New Pluralism." In F. Hesselbein, M. Goldsmith, and I. Sommerville (eds.), *Leading Beyond the Walls.* San Francisco, Jossey-Bass, 1999, p. 9.

6. David Satcher, M.D., assistant secretary for health and surgeon general of the United States, in a speech to the U.S. Coalition for Healthier Cities and Communities and the National Civic League, Washington, D.C., 1998.

7. Hawken, P. "Five Signs of the Coming Revolution." Utne Reader, Nov.–Dec. 2000.

8. Van Gelder, S. "A Culture Gets Creative." *Yes, A Journal of Positive Futures* (interview with P. Ray and S. Anderson), Winter 2001, p. 15. (www.yesmagazine.org)

9. Adams, C., Pittman, M., Norris, T., and others. "A Message to America from America's Communities." Chicago: Coalition for Healthier Cities and Communities, Health Research and Educational Trust, AHA Press, 1999.

10. Ayre, Clough, and Norris (2000).

11. Morse, S. "The Morphing of Civic Organizations." *Community Magazine of the United Way of America,* vol. 3, Spring–Summer 2000, pp. 27–29.

12. Gates, C. T. "Creating a Healthy Democracy." In *Civic Index.* Denver: National Civic League, 1999.

13. Kretzmann, J. P., and McKnight, J. L. *Building Communities from the Inside Out.* Evanston, Ill.: Asset-Based Community Development Institute, Northwestern University, 1993.

14. Norris, T., and others. "Healthy People in Healthy Communities: A Dialogue Guide." Chicago: Coalition for Healthier Cities and Communities, Health Research and Educational Trust, AHA Press, 1999.

15. Kesler, J. 2001. (http://www.healthycommunities.org/healthycommunities.html)

16. Swain, D. "Measuring Progress: Community Indicators and the Quality of Life." *International Journal of Public Administration,* in press; Atkisson, A., Besleme, K., Norris, T., Van Genderen, H., and others. *The Community Indicators Handbook.* Oakland, Calif.: Redefining Progress, 1997.

Tyler Norris is president of Community Initiatives in Boulder, Colorado.

Linking Civic Engagement and Community Improvement: A Practitioner Perspective on the Communities Movement

David Swain

It may seem self-evident that constructive civic engagement usually produces community improvement and that significant community improvements usually reflect the exercise of effective civic engagement. Yet the linkage between the two is less direct and causal, and more fragmented and fragile, than might be imagined. Successfully harnessing civic engagement to achieve community improvement is difficult. However, the well-being of our citizens and the realization of our democratic ideals demand that communities across America face up to this challenge. The communities movement now emerging in the United States is seeking ways to move beyond recognizing the challenge toward more completely understanding its dynamics and identifying effective practices for use in American communities.

In the first part of this article, I examine, from a general perspective, major issues that must be addressed for the engagement-improvement linkage to work effectively. In the second part, I describe how the efforts of one community-based organization—the Jacksonville Community Council Inc. (JCCI), in Florida—has tackled these issues over twenty-six years, the successes that have resulted, and the challenges that remain. Both parts are intended to contribute to the greater understanding being sought by the communities movement.

The Big Picture

Intentional community improvement (also referred to here as positive change) occurs as a result of conscious effort on the part of individuals and institutions within the community, perhaps enhanced by intervention on the part of outsiders. America's civic culture places high value on maximizing the democratization of these conscious efforts, and the emerging communities movement is motivated by a desire to help guide communities toward putting democratized community improvement widely and effectively into practice.

NATIONAL CIVIC REVIEW, vol. 90, no. 4, Winter 2001 © Wiley Periodicals, Inc.

For such guidance to be helpful, it must help a community answer key questions in several clusters:

• *Sparking action.* How do sparks catalyze action and initiate movement toward positive change? Are these sparks usually generated by an individual, an extraordinary leader? by an institutional source? from the top down (leadership) or the bottom up (grassroots)? from a public (governmental) entity or from a private (for-profit or nonprofit) source? from internal sources or from those external to the community?

• *Maintaining momentum.* What factors most effectively stimulate movement toward positive change, creating motivation and momentum for progress? What breadth, depth, and diversity of participation are optimal? Which key individuals or institutions are essential for success? How crucial is institutional partnership or collaboration? How critical is the role of neutral convener, and what kind of institution can successfully play that role?

• *Facilitating the process.* What approaches to and methods of involvement, participation, or engagement are most effective in facilitating a process that moves toward positive change? Is the most effective emphasis placed on confrontational conflict resolution, on collaborative consensus building, or on some combination? What roles do collective learning, planning, and advocacy most effectively play? How can tools such as visioning, goal and priority setting, and outcome measurement through community indicators and performance measures be used most effectively?

• *Institutionalizing change.* What kind of organizational arrangement is most effective in institutionalizing positive change so that it becomes part of the new status quo? What is the most effective role here for local government? for a neutral convener? for citizen advocates? for other public and private institutions and interest groups? for collaboration among some or all of these entities?

The sections that follow explain and consider these clustered questions in detail.

Sparking Action

The source of the spark for community change is an oft-debated issue that need not be rehashed by the communities movement. The movement's most useful guidance to a community is to alert it to possible sources—individual and institutional, leadership and grassroots, public and private, internal and external. It can also help by encouraging advocates for community engagement and improvement to search diligently for a potential catalyst and to communicate with it early, seeking to fan any initial flame.

This sort of guidance can be useful to the extent that activists have done their homework to assess the civic assets available in their community. Such asset assessment identifies movers and shakers, whether individuals or institutions, at various levels and in various arenas of community life, as well as how things get done in the community. The communities movement can help by strengthening a community's ability to assess civic assets fully and accurately.

In practice, issues needing community improvement are not generalized or generic. Each tends to be specific to a certain set of concerns and interests, individuals and institutions, and often to a particular geographic area. Promoting civic engagement and community improvement may thus require application of a unique approach, for each community issue, in each community, in relation to sparking action, maintaining momentum, facilitating the process, and institutionalizing change. The communities movement can help by alerting communities that the devil is in the details.

Maintaining Momentum

Sparks may fly concerning a community issue, but they may soon fizzle unless the timing is right to put the issue on the community's agenda for serious consideration, in-depth dialogue, decision making, and action. Most communities continuously face multiple issues but are able to focus on only a few at a time in any depth. Thus issues compete for the community's attention. In few communities is this competitive process controllable by a specific individual or institution (although in most communities, an individual or institution may have greater or lesser influence over particular issues or over the agenda-setting process itself). Consequently, community agenda setting often appears to occur mysteriously and unpredictably.

Although timing is everything, fanning an initial spark may still help to increase the salience of an issue to the point that it emerges as a priority on the community agenda. Maintaining momentum on an issue that has emerged onto the agenda requires quick and effective activist response.

One way a community responds to an emerging issue is through an old-boy network of public and private power brokers, often supported by large institutions such as a local government, chamber of commerce, or university. This approach precludes meaningful civic engagement, so the communities movement is clearly seeking to promote a democratized alternative.

The Neutral Convener Role. Civic engagement may occasionally seem to spring up spontaneously. However, to be sustained in a community, it must be nurtured, facilitated, organized, and institutionalized. Communities seeking to link civic engagement with community improvement are coming to recognize that one essential ingredient for success is the availability of a "neutral convener." Most institutions and entities in a community are not neutral since each one's mission promotes a particular set of concerns or interests in the community. The chamber of commerce supports business interests, a church is a religious institution, a human services agency addresses various human needs, and a civic club exists primarily for member fellowship and networking.

Local government might appear to represent an exception. However, for at least two reasons it cannot, in many cases, serve effectively as the community's neutral convener. First, the geographic and functional fragmentation of local government precludes its effectively playing an overall community role, in many urban areas at least. Second, many people these days perceive themselves to be in a *we-they* relationship with government, seeing government as just another self-interested institution beholden to many political interests—but one with extraordinary power over important aspects of their quality of life. A neutral convener must be not only neutral but independent, trusted, and credible.

The role of neutral convener is of unique importance in linking civic engagement and community improvement because it offers an open, unbiased space in which facilitated community learning, dialogue, planning, consensus building, conflict resolution, and joint action for community improvement can take place. The bias or interest of the convener is to enable the processes of engagement and improvement so that they can flourish effectively, in whatever direction the convened community decides to take them during consideration of any specific issue.

Neutral Convener Models. Although communities in America exhibit extraordinary ingenuity in establishing creative institutional solutions, to date they have not institutionalized the neutral convener role in any commonly recognizable form. However, two models exist that are being used successfully in some communities, mostly urban, across the land.

Citizen Leagues. The impetus for the creation of citizen leagues came from the Progressive Movement in the early twentieth century, with close ties to what was then the newly established National Municipal League (the forerunner of the National Civic League), although most existing citizen leagues were founded more recently. Active citizen leagues operate in mostly urban, predominantly metropolitan areas such as Minneapolis, Cleveland, St. Louis, Seattle, Kansas City, and Jacksonville. In recent years, citizen leagues have begun to refer to themselves as "regional civic organizations," in recognition that the community they serve encompasses a large metropolitan region made up of many neighborhoods (as well as multiple local governmental jurisdictions). About fifty citizen leagues are listed on the regional civic organizations network Website (www.citizensleague.net/rco/default.htm).

Citizen leagues differ considerably among themselves, but they all function as a private, nonprofit, nonpartisan, citizen-based organization dedicated to civic engagement and community improvement. They share a mission that includes broadly based, direct involvement of individual citizens and community institutions to learn about and discuss significant community issues and to advocate for positive change. They offer a variety of engagement opportunities through community leadership development, citizen-based research studies, public forums on major issues, and direct advocacy for public policy change. As neutral conveners, citizen leagues are able, as no other entity in a community, to bring all community interests together for mutual learning, consensus building, decision making, and advocacy for community improvement.

Community Planning Councils. As organized human services philanthropy and coordinated funding of human services at the community level developed during the first half of the twentieth century, funders and providers alike saw the need to develop a community-based planning capacity to ensure logical allocation of funding to meet human needs. Many local United Ways, in particular, established either a planning department within their own organization or a stand-alone community planning council. Councils were founded as private, nonprofit organizations with a strong commitment, in their planning process, to civic engagement by both individuals and institutions. The National Association of Planning Councils currently lists about thirty-five council members, but a number of additional communities also have councillike institutions. Although some planning councils serve a rural or small-town area, most, like a citizen league, serve an urban or metropolitan area; they are located across the country in places as diverse as Sacramento, Ithaca, Dallas, Honolulu, and, again, Jacksonville (see www.communityplanning.org).

Although the focus of planning council work continues to be on human services issues, the definition of human services is constantly being stretched, as councils seek to engage in community-level planning around the closely interrelated issues of economic prosperity, social well-being, public health, clean environments, and safe neighborhoods. As the scope of community planning has expanded and the variety of interests involved in the participative planning process has increased, many a planning council, like the citizen league, has become the neutral convener in its community.

Most communities in America lack a recognized neutral convener entity such as a citizen league or planning council. Increasingly, many are turning to an existing citizen league or planning council, seeking advice on how to establish the neutral convener role in the community. In addition, the community foundation in a locality may expand its role to include aspects of community planning, civic engagement, and neutral convening.

Without some sort of neutral convener entity in place, a community lacks an institutional vehicle to stimulate and motivate civic engagement toward community improvement, except to the extent that traditional interest groups and institutions can marshal support for their particular issues. Without such a vehicle, a community lacks the capacity to address important momentum questions, such as who should be involved; what kind of partnership or collaboration is needed; and what kind of process should be used to address, through civic engagement, the major issues of concern to the entire community.

Facilitating the Process

Citizens in the United States have used a variety of methods to create or facilitate change in a community, everything from writing letters to the editor to legislative lobbying and engaging in mass rallies or protest. Civic engagement, as a means of achieving community improvement, suggests a process, located somewhere in the middle range of the spectrum, that is group-oriented, orderly, ongoing, open, structured, in-depth, and ultimately effective. Such a process is consistent with the thinking emerging from the communities movement.

Conflict and Consensus Models. Beyond these commonalities, questions emerge. For example, to be effective must civic engagement be confrontational, assuming that many community issues are deeply conflictual and can be resolved only through conflict resolution? Or may the process be collaborative, assuming that a broad consensus exists in most communities about most major issues and that a consensus-building process usually can produce an acceptable decision for community improvement?

Although few of those working in communities would tend to answer these questions categorically one way or the other, major models describe processes consistent with each approach. The community organization model, especially as articulated and practiced by Saul Alinsky, assumes a conflictual environment and prescribes a confrontational approach. The civil rights and antiwar movements of the 1960s and 1970s seemed to confirm the validity and necessity of a conflictual approach to community change. Even some community action agencies experimented, during those years, with community organization as part of the federally funded War on Poverty.

Beginning in the 1980s and continuing to the present, a more consensus-oriented perception of community environments has emerged. Some of the factors that have influenced this shift, or been influenced by it, are the increasing percentage of minorities in the middle class, diminished housing segregation, the lifting of desegregation orders as federal courts declared public school districts "unitary," the flourishing of conservatism, widespread economic prosperity, and the supplanting of class and racial concepts rooted in conflict with others based on acceptance and even celebration of diversity.

Today, some argue that consensus can be achieved because mainstream America really does agree on most core values and important issues. Others would only partially agree with this view, pointing out major issues on which consensus clearly does not exist in many communities (growth management, social welfare, race relations) as well as the reality that in many communities a socioeconomic and geographic chasm is rapidly widening between the well-off and the poor.

The processes used by citizen leagues and planning councils are grounded largely on a consensus-building model. Yet, as they have sought to play the neutral convener role, some have found the need to use an alternative, conflict resolution model as well. This conflict-oriented process differs from confrontational community organization by relying on methods more closely related to consensus building—dialogue among all affected interests, mediation, negotiation, and sometimes arbitration—rather than mass protest and public demand for change.

Community Improvement Model. The shift toward consensus-oriented civic engagement for community improvement has given rise to new methods and, more important, to articulation of an overall model for community improvement. Although this model is nowhere consciously institutionalized, it roughly reflects the actual processes that communities use, with myriad unique permutations, to achieve positive community change in a consensus-oriented environment. It is based on systems theory, presuming that community improvement is an ongoing, iterative process resulting usually in short-term incremental changes that can build on one another over time. Applying such a model to a predominantly conflictual community environment is difficult because the dynamics are less predictable and change, when it occurs, may be abrupt and large-scale.

The model can be diagrammed as shown in Figure 1.

Vision. Theoretically (but rarely in practice, since no existing community begins with a tabula rasa), the process begins with community visioning to think about, identify, and reach consensus on overriding values and goals for the community's well-being. Many communities have undertaken visioning exercises in recent years, and some citizen leagues and planning councils have contributed directly to these efforts. Some communities have followed through to make specific plans and take specific actions based on their vision, while other vision statements have languished on the shelf.

Indicators. A growing number of communities are discovering the value of defining and tracking measurable indicators of community well-being. Indicators offer a way to articulate the values of the vision in terms of real, measurable community outcomes. For instance, an indicator of the public high school graduation rate might help illuminate the status of a community's visionary goal of having a well-educated citizenry (emulating Lake Wobegon). Some indicator projects have been initiated and operated by local governments, but most have been developed by private nonprofit organizations (a chamber of commerce, a United Way, a health care institution, or other). Most citizen leagues and planning councils have become involved in measuring community indicators, which are being used to inform citizens and decision makers and to guide efforts toward community improvement. However, an indicator itself (for instance, a declining graduation rate) cannot

Figure 1. Community Improvement Model

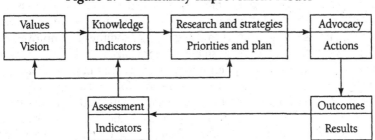

lead a community directly to action for improvement because it reveals neither the cause behind the status and trend of the indicator nor what must be done for improvement. Thus additional, intermediate steps are necessary in the community improvement process.

Whether or not the process moves on to these additional steps depends on the dynamics of sparking action and maintaining momentum, as we have already discussed. For many community issues, a vision statement and indicators may exist for years but be largely ignored on the community agenda, because their status is considered satisfactory or the status quo is too entrenched to be susceptible to positive change. At some point, however, a combination of an activist leader, an institutional commitment, and perhaps an unforeseen event or crisis may emerge to elevate an issue onto the agenda. At that point, the timing is right for planning, advocacy, and action.

Planning. Many institutions (local government, institutions of higher education, trade associations, interest groups) address community improvement issues by conducting research, planning, strategizing, and prioritizing of issues and solutions. A neutral convener entity can play a unique role by conducting such an activity using methods of citizen engagement aimed at achieving improvement beneficial to the entire community. Citizen leagues and planning councils use a variety of methods, some (public workshops and forums, citizen-based research and study processes, facilitated planning processes) relying directly on a vision statement and indicators. Typically, these processes directly involve a diverse mix of citizens and stakeholders. The results are often a recommendation or plan directed at specific community institutions and calling for specific community-improvement actions.

Advocacy. Once a recommendation or plan is in place, advocacy is usually needed to secure authoritative action and commitment of necessary resources. Such advocacy occurs through the political and budgeting processes of local government, or lobbying and marketing by an interest group, or the decision-making process of businesses and nonprofit organizations. Once again, a neutral convener entity can play a unique role by marshalling the influence of citizens on behalf of the community's overall well-being. Many citizen leagues and planning councils are heavily involved in citizen-based advocacy work.

Results. If all goes well with the advocacy process, responsible institutions respond with action, producing results that can be measured. The annual budget cycle used by most public and private institutions relies primarily on twelve-month program results, but measuring broader, longer-term outcomes is also important to assess overall community improvement.

Assessment. Sometimes assessment is formalized and sometimes not, especially in relation to long-term impact. A community that has developed indicators of well-being has a valuable tool for measuring progress. The same indicators that were useful to guide planning early in the process are used later on to measure the degree of success. Through the iterative feedback loop, the results of the assessment can then be applied again for the next round of planning. They might also lead to some rethinking of the indicators or possibly even to a refinement of the vision. Annually published indicator report cards yield valuable trend-line (and, in some cases, community goal) information that can be used for assessment, as well as future planning, indicator choices, and visioning. A neutral convener entity can provide such a report card from an overall community improvement perspective, one that other institutions in the community may lack. Some citizen leagues and planning councils periodically publish formal indicator documents in print or online.

Capacities Required. Regardless of the institution or organization engaging in all of this activity, certain organizational capacities are required to facilitate successful linkage of civic engagement and community improvement—at a minimum:

- *Credibility.* A citizen-based community improvement effort may have little success if its lead institution lacks credibility in the community. This is one of the primary assets of a neutral convener entity and helps to explain why identification or development of an effective convener entity is so important for a community desiring to improve itself through citizen engagement. As has been suggested, some local governments may be able to pass the trust test and serve as a credible neutral convener. However, most communities may be better served by an independent, private, nonprofit, citizen-based organization.
- *Planning skills.* Conducting any of the processes in the community improvement model, from visioning through assessment, requires access to expert staff skills in research, planning, and writing. The integrity and usefulness of the results depend heavily on the depth of research, logic of planning, and clarity of written communications produced by the effort.
- *Facilitation skills.* Equally, success depends heavily on the staff skills of group facilitation, consensus building, and, if necessary, conflict resolution being brought to bear through the process.
- *Open outreach.* Even with superb planning and facilitation resources, citizen engagement cannot be successful without effective outreach to ensure that a broad diversity of citizens and relevant stakeholder institutions and interest groups are brought within the tent to participate directly together.
- *Financial resources.* Neither effective citizen engagement nor significant community improvement—nor successful linkage—can be accomplished through volunteer effort alone. A substantial commitment of financial resources is necessary to make available adequate staffing, meeting and office facilities and amenities, duplicating and printing, online expenses, supplies, and the like. Ideally, a community improvement process should be able to rely for funding on a range of public and private sources, each of which understands the benefits accruing to itself by supporting an overall community improvement effort.

Institutionalizing Change. In the community improvement model, change is institutionalized by leaders and institutions in response to the recommendations and plans advocated for and supported by the community. In some cases, a single existing institution may clearly be the proper implementer of a recommendation or plan. In some other cases, a newly created institution may be necessary. However, given the complex interrelationship among issues and organizations, many significant community issues can be addressed only by multiple institutions working together.

In recent years, partnerships, coalitions, and collaboratives have become popular as an organizational vehicle to channel and enhance the interrelationship necessary for success. As a result, planning and advocacy efforts often become preoccupied with issues of institutional development. Along the way, interinstitutional entities have proliferated to the extent that not-so-humorous jests are heard about the need to create a coalition of coalitions. At the community level, establishing a coalition of existing nonprofits is sometimes viewed as a positive alternative to creating a new nonprofit organization in competition with others, although this still requires new organization building.

Even though developing these complex organizational entities may be necessary and even desirable, it greatly complicates the process of institutionalizing change. From one perspective, this need not be relevant to civic engagement. After all, the community has spoken with its recommendations and plans. The responsibility to act now lies with the institutions toward which the recommendations and plans are directed. From another perspective, however, ensuring that ongoing civic engagement takes place until change is successfully institutionalized makes sense. Most communities have experienced the letdown of seeing a good plan sit on the shelf gathering dust. The citizen advocacy process can help ensure that recommendations and plans are actually implemented.

Embracing the latter perspective draws civic engagement deeply into the complexity of institutional development. As with other aspects of civic engagement, this process calls for facilitation from a neutral convener.

Three points are important in this regard. First, citizen-based implementation is not really implementation. It is advocacy, using citizen influence, directed to the institutions designated to implement, to ensure that they are aware of what they are being asked to implement and that they respond constructively. Advocacy by citizens can sometimes fall into the trap of their attempting to implement directly themselves, either because they are so invested in the success of their recommendation or plan or because the responsible agency manages to co-opt them into doing its job.

Second, implementing recommendations or plans requiring new institutional development (either a single, new organization or a collaborative entity of existing organizations) may bog down unless a lead or convening organization is clearly designated—some entity that citizens can hold responsible for starting the institutional development process.

Third, successful implementation of a recommendation or plan calling for development of a partnership, coalition, or collaborative may require extended facilitation of some combination of consensus building and conflict resolution to overcome turf issues and negotiate an acceptable relationship among the existing organizations.

What role can a neutral convener entity effectively play in such a situation? As a facilitator of civic engagement toward implementation of community recommendations or plans, it can provide staff support to citizen-based advocacy efforts. In addition, it may be uniquely capable of convening existing organizations charged with new institution building, whether for a stand-alone organization or a coalition.

The Jacksonville Perspective

The Jacksonville Community Council Inc. is a private nonprofit organization established in 1975 to play the role of neutral convener to link civic engagement and community improvement in the Jacksonville, Florida, metropolitan area. The impetus for the founding of JCCI came as part of the aftermath of the good-government reform movement that led, in 1968, to consolidation of the City of Jacksonville with Duval County. Six years after the consolidated government was inaugurated, reform-minded leaders from business and government agreed that the new structure and professionalized public service were working well but that the community lacked a mechanism to develop civic leadership and engage citizens on important community issues. The following year, the reform movement spawned two new nonprofit organizations, one for community leadership development (Leadership Jacksonville, Inc.) and the other as a vehicle to engage these leaders and other citizens to learn about community issues and advocate for improvement (JCCI).

The initial organizational structure and programmatic content for JCCI were derived from two models known to the reformers in different ways: the planning council model and the citizen league model. Organizationally, JCCI was actually reincorporated from a previous organization, the Jacksonville Community Planning Council, which had been doing human services planning under various names for the local United Way since 1915. The Planning Council had already established patterns of involving citizen volunteers and stakeholder agencies on study committees concerned with human services issues.

The citizen league model was borrowed largely intact from the Minnesota Citizens League, which, having been founded in the 1940s, was already a mature organization with well-developed programs, especially a citizen-based process of studying community issues and issuing reports with recommendations for improvement.

Thus JCCI went into business having grafted together what are still the two most prominent models for the neutral convener role. Today, JCCI remains the only organization in the country consciously organized around this dual heritage.

JCCI began modestly but has grown substantially as various opportunities, consistent with the initial mission, brought new programs, additional staff, and a greater number of volunteers. Today, the organization has a staff of twelve, a budget of about $750,000, and an individual membership of about seven hundred. Major funding sources include the United Way (still), the Consolidated City of Jacksonville, corporate contributors, and contract revenues.

Here are the organization's recent and current major programs (see www.jcci.org for more information).

Study and Implementation Process. JCCI conducts two major studies each year, one on a human services issue (funded by United Way), the other on a community improvement issue (funded partly by the consolidated government and partly from corporate contributions). The process used was developed by citizen leagues. Study issues are selected each year through a process with extensive and intensive citizen involvement guided by specific selection criteria. One important criterion relates to timing and the status of each issue on the community agenda. With more than fifty studies completed to date, the range of issues addressed has become broad. Most studies have dealt with specific substantive issues, such as growth management, teen pregnancy, emergency preparedness, and the quality of public education. A few have tackled issues related to the community improvement process in which JCCI itself is involved, including studies on the local election process, public dialogue, and community leadership.

Each study offers a structured, facilitated learning and consensus-building process for volunteer committees of between forty and eighty people meeting weekly from October to April. Participation is open to all citizens, whether JCCI members or not. Invited expert resource people make presentations; staff share background research with committee members; written findings are drafted by staff and reviewed, revised, and approved by committee members; committee members draw conclusions from their findings and develop recommendations from their conclusions; and the resulting study report is printed and released at a public luncheon.

Following the release of each study, a facilitated implementation process begins, through which volunteer advocates (mostly those who served on the study committee) inform relevant decision makers about the recommendations and advocate for their implementation. This process typically lasts about two years, but in a few cases it has gone on much longer. In recent years, several studies have included recommendations on institution building. Implementation task forces have had mixed success in developing new organizations and coalitions, depending primarily on the dynamics of organizational turf and commitment of resources.

Indicators. JCCI currently operates two indicators projects. The Quality of Life Indicators Project began in 1985, pioneering the concept of community indicators for the nation and the world. JCCI partners with the chamber of commerce and consolidated government on this project. Over the years, with staff facilitation and research support citizen volunteers have designed the project, selected the indicators, reviewed each year's update document, set a target (community goal) for each indicator, set priorities among the indicators, and identified important linkages among indicators. JCCI uses these indicators extensively in conjunction with its study process; many other public and private entities use them for purposes of strategic planning, resource development, budgeting, and resource allocation.

The Community Agenda Indicators Project was started in 1995, at the request of United Way, to produce a set of human services indicators it could use as a guide for allocation of funding. The process for this project of involving citizen volunteers, supported by staff research and facilitation, has been similar to that used for the quality-of-life project.

Human Services Council. A 1981 JCCI study that recommended better coordination among human services funders resulted in creation of the Human Services Council (HSC). Its "partners" include all major public and private funders in the Northeast Florida region. Since the HSC's inception, JCCI has provided staffing services, supporting a variety of human services planning and coordination efforts consistent with its role as a planning council. The HSC members have formally adopted the community agenda indicators as a guide for planning and resource allocation.

Conflict Resolution. By the early 1990s, JCCI had come to recognize that not all community issues could be addressed successfully through the consensus-based process of citizen-based studies, indicator tracking, and community planning. It therefore designed a program to offer intensive training for citizen volunteers in community conflict resolution. More than six hundred individuals underwent this training. Soon, many of them were becoming actively involved on their own in resolving community disputes. JCCI became formally involved in two ways, first by facilitating a major conflict resolution process to design a sex education curriculum for the public schools, and second by managing a neighborhood conflict resolution project for the consolidated government. Volunteer graduates of the training program conducted all of the actual conflict resolution activities. By the late 1990s, JCCI felt it had played out its useful role in this area and sought to spin off the conflict resolution activities. For a number of reasons, the spin-off did not occur; Jacksonville now has no formal community conflict resolution project.

JCCI Forward. Over the years, JCCI was discouraged by limited success in involving younger citizens in its volunteer activities. In 2000, a major effort was begun to overcome this limitation. Recognizing the need to nurture and stimulate emerging leaders (beyond the limited capacity of the Leadership Jacksonville program), JCCI convened a group of young people to discuss the possibilities, and JCCI Forward took off on its own as a new program. The program has involved almost seven hundred young leaders (some of whom are also JCCI members) in a miniversion of the study process, public forums, and social activities. The effort has proved that young people are eager for civic engagement and volunteer if given an appropriate opportunity, and it has given JCCI a major new role in developing the next generation of Jacksonville's leadership.

Five O'clock Forum. Volunteers looking for a shorter-term volunteer opportunity than the study process convinced JCCI of the need to allow citizens to gather for dialogue and learning about community issues. The Five O'clock Forum project offers periodic public forums, facilitated by volunteers, on issues that are hot and controversial at the moment. Most citizen leagues offer similar opportunities.

Contract Projects. Public and private institutions in Northeast Florida have learned that JCCI offers an ideal venue to bring major issues for facilitated consensus-building study and planning processes. Thus, JCCI has become not just a self-appointed neutral convener but also the neutral convener of choice for the entire community. Some contract projects have used modified versions of the JCCI study and implementation process. Others have used a facilitated stakeholder planning process. The range of issues brought to JCCI through contracts is quite broad: studies on fair housing, the local sex trade, needle exchange and planning processes for implementation of a specific treatment model for those dually diagnosed with drug-abuse and mental-health problems, and preservation of a historic golf course clubhouse as a center for ecoheritage learning and tourism.

In twenty-six years, JCCI has earned a solid reputation for credibility, impartiality, and technical excellence in its work. This track record has made it possible for the organization to become trusted and acknowledged as the Jacksonville area's recognized neutral convener, the one place in Northeast Florida that consciously seeks to improve the entire community through effective civic engagement.

This reputation has not been easily earned and is not easily maintained. Repeatedly, recommendations from JCCI's studies are aimed at major funders and supporters; not all are kindly received. This reality makes annual budgeting and fundraising a sensitive and challenging endeavor. It has also led JCCI to make a concerted effort to maintain a close working relationship with its major partners: United Way, the consolidated government, and the chamber of commerce. At the same time, JCCI has had to remain vigilant to maintain an independent, impartial position in the community so that its credibility and trust are not jeopardized. Ongoing efforts to maintain strong, non-earmarked financial support from the corporate community have helped in this regard. JCCI walks a tightrope, but so far the organization's credibility has been secure enough to maintain the balancing act.

JCCI faces several additional challenges, notably reaching out more successfully to segments of the population that are not likely to become involved in community-level civic engagement, especially minorities and the poor;

"marketing" the organization's name and mission more successfully to the many for whom civic engagement and community improvement are unfamiliar concepts; measuring tangibly the difference that JCCI's efforts have made over the years to improve the community's quality of life; and taking full advantage of rapidly emerging and evolving computer and telecommunications technologies to enhance JCCI's civic engagement activities.

JCCI's approach to linking civic engagement and community improvement is unique, having developed as it did within a particular civic environment during a particular period of time. Many other communities are successfully making the linkage in substantially different ways. Yet the JCCI experience offers a valuable lesson for consideration by other communities, a model for possible adaptation, and food for thought on the part of the emerging communities movement.

David Swain is associate director of the Jacksonville Community Council Inc. (JCCI) in Jacksonville, Florida.

Investment-Based Business Plans for Human Service Delivery: A New Model Takes Shape in Des Moines, Iowa

Becky Miles-Polka

Numerous difficulties attend efforts to bring human service professionals and neighborhood residents together to address community needs. Individuals who can successfully navigate among local service systems, government sectors, and neighborhoods appear to be a critical element for success. This article focuses on a community process under way in Polk County, Iowa, which brings together leaders in early childhood, housing, and local neighborhoods. The goal of the initiative is to design and implement a new neighborhood-based service model that is premised on rethinking the relationships among citizens and the social services that support child and family well-being.

Many of the leading causes of death in the United States are attributable to lifestyle and behavioral factors.[1] Alcohol, tobacco, and other drug use; improper diet and inadequate exercise; extent and nature of motor vehicle operation; and use of firearms are among the most important of these factors.

Certain of the behaviors associated with increased mortality rate are linked to social variables such as income and education level. By providing economic opportunities, strong education systems, and hope in the future, healthy communities support healthy people. Increasingly, throughout this country and abroad, citizens and leaders have come to recognize the importance of collaborative effort in creating a healthier community. Both the theory and practice in this area continue to evolve, increasing our knowledge of what is possible.

One of the essential prerequisites for fostering collective change is that citizens and leaders have a continuing opportunity to discuss the future of their

Note: Special thanks to these groups and organizations: Capitol East Neighborhood Association; Charlie Bruner, director of the Child and Family Policy Center; Early Childhood Partnership; Greater Des Moines Leadership Coalition; Healthy Polk 2010; HSPA Housing Coalition; Human Services Planning Alliance; Making Connections Neighborhood Circles.

community. As our experience in Polk County has taught us, values and practices such as trust, mutual respect, shared learning, reflection, and optimism are also needed as efforts are made to promote alignment across sectors. In concert with many others, our organization, the Human Services Planning Alliance (HSPA), has made progress in such areas as juvenile justice, health, human services, and education. We continue to build social capital by working with faith-based and grassroots neighborhood organizations. The changing demographics of our community have created a new dimension to this work as we blend capacity development with inclusive participation.

Human Service Planning Goes to Business School

Located in the heart of Iowa, Polk County is the most populated of the state's ninety-nine counties. It is home to the capital, Des Moines, and also includes within its boundaries the most rapidly growing metropolitan area in the state, West Des Moines. Combining rural with urban environments, Polk County boasts a population that is rapidly becoming a broad cultural and ethnic mix as immigrants and refugees—most recently from Mexico, Central America, Sudan, and Bosnia—seek new opportunities in the country's heartland.

Community planning activities are not new to Des Moines. Organized planning has been conducted here for the past two decades, but until recently it was fragmented among some twenty groups. Over the last several years, a consensus was reached concerning the need for a new model of human service planning (Figure 1). Progressive leadership within the human service sector and the increasing embrace of performance-based models by local, state, and national funding sources were important factors in this development. In 1998, after a lengthy process that included a communitywide facilitated meeting, HSPA was formed, creating an opportunity to consolidate existing efforts and improve cross-sector planning. The original twenty groups have been organized into five planning clusters: early childhood, youth, health, housing and neighborhoods, and workforce development.

These are HSPA's core functions:

- Fostering dialogue and collaboration through inclusion and active participation of representative community leadership, consumers, and advocates
- Facilitating priority setting and issue identification, using broad-based public opinion
- Ensuring collection and dissemination of relevant data for planning
- Aligning and streamlining existing planning efforts
- Fostering coordination and information sharing among funding sources
- Developing and implementing appropriate evaluation systems
- Influencing public policy by offering elected officials guidance on human service priorities

Figure 1. Polk County Change Model

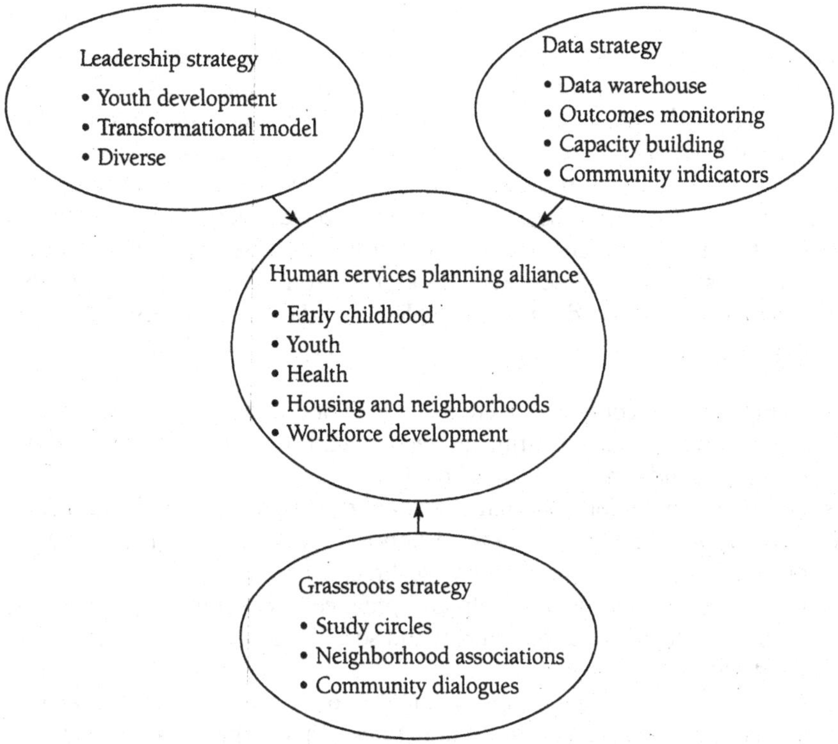

Leadership strategy
- Youth development
- Transformational model
- Diverse

Data strategy
- Data warehouse
- Outcomes monitoring
- Capacity building
- Community indicators

Human services planning alliance
- Early childhood
- Youth
- Health
- Housing and neighborhoods
- Workforce development

Grassroots strategy
- Study circles
- Neighborhood associations
- Community dialogues

There are thirty community constituencies in HSPA, from the government, business, community, health, education, and juvenile justice sectors. The alliance went through a priority-setting process in 1999 and identified three areas where efforts will be focused over the next several years. Work is under way to develop business plans in each of these priority areas:

1. Early childhood: improve school readiness, improve maternal and child health, and reduce child abuse and neglect
2. Housing: increase the availability of affordable housing for low-income residents and improve housing conditions and public infrastructure in neighborhoods
3. Self-sufficiency: empower job seekers to secure employment and strengthen the connection between temporary economic assistance and preparation for work-related self-sufficiency

Business plan development for each priority area is intended to identify opportunities for cross-sector collaboration in planning, design, and implementation. Representatives from the sectors meet regularly to share updates on progress in designing and implementing the plans.

Early Childhood Business Plan

The comprehensive business plan that was developed for the early childhood priority area illustrates the principles underlying HSPAs approach. The plan is based on systematic analysis of community and investment strategies that are conducive to the positive development and well-being of children through the age of five years. For example, it is well accepted that the environment and care a child receives in the first three years of life significantly affects brain development. Failure to ensure that children receive adequate care during this period results in direct and indirect social costs. A targeted program that delivers needed services in these areas is a social investment for which it is possible to calculate an estimated return. The plan identifies four universal needs for young children:

- Competent and confident parenting (at least one, and preferably two, parent figures who provide nurturing, protection, and stimulation and with whom the child bonds and forms attachments)
- Health and nutrition (adequate food and exercise for physical and mental growth, protection against and response to disease and injury, and early detection and treatment of special health care needs)
- Guidance and instruction (help and practice in developing motor skills, preliteracy cognitive development, and socialization with adults and other children)
- Constant, stable, and appropriate supervision (continuous adult oversight and support that enables the child to safely explore the environment)[2]

The plan describes significant costs and poor outcomes that are linked to failing to meet these universal early childhood needs. Charlie Bruner, of the Child and Family Policy Center in Des Moines and principal investigator for HSPAs early childhood business plan, notes that "social costs include public expenditures for compensatory and remediation services, for welfare/public assistance programs, and for public protection services; and lost economic activity and a reduced overall tax base."[3] The annual state investment in early childhood programs in Iowa is $113 million. By comparison, total state-level spending on incarceration, public law enforcement, juvenile justice, and entitlement programs is more than $2.2 billion. Bruner estimates that for Polk County alone tax expenditures in these areas amount to $155 million, which does not include lost economic activity and reduced tax revenue.[4]

The early childhood business plan outlines opportunities for investment in Polk County in each of the four critical need areas. Much like a standard business plan, the early childhood plan identifies investment opportunities, target markets, product lines, and estimated returns on investment. Best practices were identified through research and input from local experts in the field.

Documentation for the business plan was submitted to a national auditing firm, RSM McGladrey, which verified the accuracy of the data, assessed the methodology and logic model, and surveyed the existing research on early childhood development and service needs. A recommendation was made to implement the plan in stages.

Two product lines were identified for the health and nutrition area: financial access to health care and access to a medical home that provides primary and preventive health care. The plan estimates that six thousand to eight thousand children may not be receiving comprehensive primary and preventive care in Polk County. Research has demonstrated a return on investment ranging from two to one to as high as ten to one for specific prevention-oriented health services such as prenatal health care, immunization, WIC services, and early detection of health issues.[5]

Healthy Polk 2010, our local health planning initiative, made recommendations on best practices for primary and preventive care for children. A neighborhood-based system of family-centered, culturally competent health centers with linkage to community support systems was envisioned. Recently, we received a Robert Wood Johnson Foundation matching grant, along with local dollars to move toward this goal. Work is under way to expand a small free clinic serving a primarily Spanish-speaking population into a comprehensive neighborhood health center. We also have significant local and state dollars focusing on outreach and community capacity building for SCHIP (State Children's Health Insurance Program) and Medicaid enrollment.

Product lines in the other critical areas include home visiting programs, enriched preschool, and quality developmentally appropriate childcare. Similar returns on investment have been demonstrated for child care, family support programming, and enriched preschool. A 1998 publication by the RAND Corporation[6] on early childhood programs is an excellent reference for more information on program models and calculation of return.

Figure 2 illustrates the concept of identifying "target markets" in the early childhood business plan.

The annual cost to meet the needs identified for children in the "market" portion of Figure 2 (eligibility determined by key risk factors) is estimated to be $27 million. The task of securing and realigning existing resources to meet these needs is clearly challenging. However, with $155 million being spent annually on remediation and other social services, a compelling case can be made that a positive net return could be realized by meeting these health needs up front. It will take a committed group of local leaders and investors with a long-range view to implement this plan. Results may not be seen for a decade, or even a generation. A new way of doing business is needed to undertake this effort, and the assumptions guiding current programs, services, and funding streams must be rethought.

Figure 2. Polk County Early Childhood Business Plan

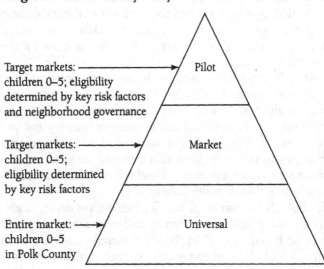

Target markets: ————→ Pilot
children 0–5; eligibility
determined by key risk factors
and neighborhood governance

Target markets: ————→ Market
children 0–5;
eligibility determined
by key risk factors

Entire market: ————→ Universal
children 0–5
in Polk County

Products for markets:
• Quality child care
• Family support and home visiting programs
• SCHIP, medical home, nutrition support
• Enriched preschool

Housing Business Plan

The housing business plan for Polk County is results-oriented and focused on outcomes:

• Safe, affordable housing for individuals and families
• Stable and self-sufficient individuals and families
• Safe, stable neighborhood environment

As with the early childhood plan, investments in specific product areas are assessed in the housing plan. These areas include:

• Market housing (housing of choice when individuals have the income means to obtain or retain housing)
• Assisted housing (housing that requires economic assistance or services to ensure family stability and self-sufficiency)
• Transitional housing (housing with support services to facilitate movement of homeless or nearly homeless individuals and families to a more permanent arrangement within twenty-four months)
• Shelter (overnight accommodations on an emergency basis of up to thirty days or a middle term of up to ninety days)

A situational analysis has been conducted and final recommendations for communitywide strategies and investment needs are near completion.

Keeping on Task: Integrating Business Plans

Under the leadership of the HSPA, work has begun on a pilot project for the first phase of the early childhood business plan. This project is to demonstrate how the products identified in the plan improve conditions for children and their families and better integrate childhood services with those in the other four clusters (housing, workforce development, youth development, and health).

Representatives from the housing and early childhood sectors were brought together to consider a joint effort. The group considered a variety of geographic locations; on the basis of local data and knowledge of existing neighborhood infrastructure, two neighborhoods located in the city core were initially selected. As part of another project, Des Moines was chosen as one of twenty-two communities nationwide to participate in the Annie E. Casey Foundation's Neighborhood Transformation/Family Development Initiative.[7] Casey Foundation staff are working in Des Moines, supporting family-strengthening strategies throughout the community and in targeted neighborhoods. The Casey Foundation has also designated the two neighborhoods chosen by HSPA as targeted neighborhoods for their initiative.

Ultimately, because of local assets, only one neighborhood was selected. Capitol East is located immediately east of the state capitol. It is an officially designated city neighborhood; the Capitol View Neighborhood Association was formed in 1989. Capitol East is home to a new elementary school, built to consolidate enrollment from two older schools in the neighborhood. The school was the first to be built in Des Moines with revenue from a recent 1 percent sales tax increase, implemented to fund school repair and redesign throughout the county. Eighty percent of children who attend Capitol View Elementary School qualify for free or reduced lunch. The school has a 43 percent mobility rate (the percentage of students who come and go within a school year).

Representatives of HSPA and the Capitol East Neighborhood Association identified areas of mutual interest, and an agreement was made to conduct a more inclusive dialogue. The Communities Movement Project (explained in the article by Kesler and O'Connor in this issue) offered an opportunity to extend these discussions. Capitol East stakeholders were among the individuals and organizations invited to participate in the regional dialogue conducted in Des Moines as part of the Communities Movement Project.

The broad constituency invited to the forum included neighborhood residents; human service, health, housing, family support, and city and county staff; private developers; representatives from faith communities; and school personnel. Participants were asked to develop a collective vision of the future for children and families in Capitol East.

One thing the group identified was a need for an early childhood center of excellence based on a family-focused model. In the scenario discussed, neighborhood leaders would guide development of such a center with support provided by HSPA. Also as part of the visioning process, participants considered how to make use of available city-owned land. For the past several years, the city of Des Moines has been acquiring property near the new school in the Capitol View neighborhood with the intention of building affordable housing. A result of the dialogue was that the city might be willing to consider alternative uses for this property.

Prior to the Communities Movement dialogue organized by the National Civic League (NCL) and the Coalition for Healthier Cities and Communities (CHCC), neighborhood residents had been meeting with key city personnel and HSPA staff to assess the possibility of developing intergenerational service programs and combining community services in a single location. This process has required, and benefited from, the continued involvement of neighborhood residents. Neighborhood leaders have actively voiced concern when partners seek to move things along too quickly or make assumptions about the collective vision of the neighborhood. Once consensus is reached in these discussions, the participants in the regional dialogue convened by NCL and CHCC will be gathered again, along with other neighborhood residents, to further refine the proposals.

Local Challenges

A number of other human services projects are under way in Des Moines. Much of the local planning work that accompanies these activities is guided by healthy communities principles:

- *An asset-based approach to individuals, families, and communities.* To see what is possible, we must look for sources of strength in people and community infrastructure.
- *A broad definition of health.* A context for health is nested in community, far beyond our traditional definitions of individual or population health.
- *A common vision for an ideal future.* Healthy communities deliberately engage a broad constituency in creating and owning a shared vision supported by a core set of community values.
- *Broad participation in civic life.* Communities are healthier when participation in community decision making is high.
- *Leadership.* Multiple sources of capital (human, social, economic and natural) must be mobilized.

As noted elsewhere in this issue, there are a number of theoretical frameworks (among others, those articulated by the Livable Cities, Sustainable Communities, and Whole Communities movements) that other organizations use to guide their efforts. Although the terminology may differ, there are a common set of values, purposes, and desired outcomes shared by these movements.

A Different Kind of Leader

All community change models recognize that some form of leadership is necessary to help foster vision and mobilize and sustain the work of improving community well-being. Organizational and change research has demonstrated the impact that key individuals can have in advancing change. In her research, Debra Myerson has articulated a set of leadership skills that are critical for successful transformative change. Myerson has identified specific types of individuals she calls "tempered radicals" and asserts that they are among the most skillful and effective leaders within an organization. She notes that "change agents are not just those characterized by bold visions and strategic savvy, but also those characterized by patience, persistence and resourcefulness . . . change agents are sensitive improvisers who are able to recognize and act on opportunities as they arise."[8] Her research has largely focused on individuals within organizations, but her insights are applicable to community change agents as well.

Tempered radicals must be skilled at navigating within the space between their own value set and that of the dominant culture where they reside. "Tempered radicals experience tensions between the status quo and alternatives, which can fuel organizational transformation," says Myerson. These navigational skills are of primary importance to community change agents. Individuals must be able to see outside and inside the systems they are part of. A high degree of comfort with ambivalence is an advantage. Myerson has determined that the tempered radical employs specific strategies to create change within an organization. These strategies can also be employed within community change work, across other domains and movements.

Small Wins. The tempered radical is especially skilled at having the patience to be content with incremental positive change. An essential component of this skill involves being prepared to see opportunities as they arise. Myerson notes that to be successful, a tempered radical must experiment with gently pushing to determine the degree of resistance.

Authentic, Personal Action. Typically, a tempered radical engenders a high degree of trust within the organization and with the external constituencies served. The person operates from deep personal conviction and authentically models behavior that at times challenges the culture of the status quo. Adept at both critiquing and advocating for the status quo, the change agent pursues a strategy that, according to Myerson, is far more complex than that of others who act strictly as a critic. A tempered radical operating within a system must at times go against the dominant culture within the organization to create positive community change.

Language and Negotiation Skills. The tempered radical is highly skilled at recognizing the need for modifying language to set the tone for a meaningful exchange of information and ideas. He or she must often be able to combine terminologies to convey ideas to a given constituency. This is another example of the state of tension these individuals find themselves in. For example, when called upon to articulate the case for why a hospital should make an upstream investment in the community, tempered radicals must be able to present the merits of their position in terms with which the decision makers are familiar. This might entail, for example, presenting a results-oriented business plan. But they must also understand the sociocultural determinants of health that affect the targeted group and be able to identify strategies that will be successful in that context. By employing this skill to educate others, the radical works within and models the space created by this tension. Myerson notes that unexpected allies often surface as this strategy is pursued.

More Tools

Another tool well known within organizational development and gaining momentum in community change work is the concept of appreciative inquiry (AI). Developed by David Cooperrider[9] and colleagues at the Case Western Reserve University School of Organizational Behavior, AI is an approach that is grounded in the potential of humans to create a desired future. Gervase R. Bushe describes AI as a way of "seeking new images in and among people's best intentions and noblest aspirations, attempting a collective envisioning of what the group could be at its very best."[10]

Although AI's focus is on the positive, on what works, and what can be, it doesn't attempt to ignore negativity or what already exists. This approach has specific relevance for community dialogue locally, regionally, and nationally. It also resonates clearly with practitioners of McKnight and Kretzman's[11] model of asset-based community development.

Another set of tools, developed from studying complex adaptive systems, is fairly new within community change work. Complex adaptive systems are notable for the interdependent feedback loops that connect individual elements in the system. Each element affects and is affected by the others without there being a central mechanism controlling the behavior of the system. Techniques such as "chunking" and use of minimal rules, which can be grouped under the rubric of complexity science, are especially useful when a high degree of uncertainty over outcomes exists and there is a low level of consensus on how to proceed.

Conclusion

The community change model in Polk County, Iowa, is a work in progress that is making a difference. Forming HSPA demonstrated a great deal of foresight. By strategically organizing what were loosely affiliated or unaffiliated efforts, we have begun to realize the benefits of leveraging our local resources.

Our community has been the recipient of numerous national foundation and federal grants in support of our collaborative model. In the past, a great deal of community energy was expended on competition for funding and leadership. We now have a shared forum within which to discuss possibilities and assess problems. Because of HSPA, we have been able to focus on other efforts that are critical to the long-term success of our community. We are more deliberate about inclusive grassroots involvement and development of broad-based leadership. Our capacity to be more data-driven and results-based in our planning is building, and we are becoming more skilled at mobilizing other community assets, including untapped social and human capital.

Many of the positive activities in our community would not have come about were it not for a key set of individuals in various organizations and in neighborhood leadership roles. They have the characteristics that Myerson has identified as defining tempered radicals: they are extremely trustworthy and can speak and understand the language of many constituency groups. These individuals function in the spaces among organizations, governmental agencies, and neighborhoods.

Community change work is an organic, complicated process. People want neighborhoods that are engaging, safe, and supportive for children, families, and individuals. Historically, many communities tend to draw a similar set of players around the table. But leadership exists in many places within our communities and often goes untapped. Identifying individuals who can see both inside and outside the systems and organizations within which they operate is a challenging but fundamental part of successful community change work.

Notes

1. McGinnis, J., and Foege, W. "Actual Causes of Death in the United States." *Journal of the American Medical Association*, 1993, 270 (18), 2207–2211.

2. Bruner, C. "Polk County Early Childhood Business Case Executive Summary." Des Moines, Iowa: Child and Family Policy Center, Nov. 2000.

3. Bruner (2000), p. 1.

4. Bruner (2000).

5. Bruner (2000).

6. Karoly, L., Greenwood, P., Everingham, S., Houbé, J., Kilburn, M., Rydell, P., Sanders, M., and Chiesa, J. "Investing in Our Children: What We Know and Don't Know About the Costs and Benefits of Early Childhood Interventions." Santa Monica, Calif.: RAND Corporation, 1998.

7. Annie E. Casey Foundation. "Making Connections Initiative: Neighborhood Transformation/Family Development." (Brochure.) Mar. 1999.

8. Myerson, D. "Tempered Radicals: How People Use Difference to Inspire Change at Work." Cambridge, Mass.: Harvard Business School Press, 2001, p. 9.

9. Cooperrider, D. "AI and the Conscious Evolution of Chaordic Organizations." *Appreciative Inquiry*, no. 20, Aug. 2000.

10. Bushe, G. "Five Theories of Change Embedded in Appreciative Inquiry." Presentation to the 18th Annual World Congress of Organization Development, Dublin, Ireland, July 14–18, 1998.

11. Kretzmann, J., and McKnight, J. *Building Communities from the Inside Out: A Path Toward Finding and Mobilizing a Community's Assets.* Chicago: ACTA, 1993.

Becky Miles-Polka is executive director of the Center for Healthy Communities at the Central Iowa Health System in Des Moines.

Community Indicators: Past, Present, and Future

Randa Gahin, Chris Paterson

A number of parallel efforts with a common focus (on balancing environmental, economic, and social concerns) and an emphasis on community participation emerged during the late 1980s and early 1990s. The Healthy Community and Sustainable Community movements, as well as a host of quality-of-life initiatives, are among them. All of these groups and projects share an interest in developing and using community indicators to collect data on which to base discussion and decisions. Indicators are used to illustrate current conditions, track trends over time, and identify important issues. Although the recent wave of community indicator projects has its own unique characteristics, the trend itself draws from a history of economic, social, urban, and more recently environmental indicators. The current use of indicators in community well-being movements owes a significant intellectual debt to the social indicators movement in particular, which has long advocated an expanded set of measures of human well-being beyond traditional economic indicators.[1]

Early Efforts

Modern interest in applying indicators to social and health issues can be traced to social reform efforts of the 1830s in Belgium, France, England, and the United States. Looking for ways to understand the nature of epidemics in industrial cities, physicians and statisticians began using social components of census data, collected for the first time during this period.[2] The temperance movement used public health indicators to try to prove that alcohol was the cause of numerous social problems.[3] The earliest collections of national statistics included demographic data, unemployment rates, crime rates, and consumption levels. Conflict over wages, unemployment, and the conditions of the working class in the latter third of the nineteenth century led to the creation of the U.S. Bureau of Labor, which provided some of the first social statistics gathered officially.[4]

Note: The research for this paper was supported by Sustainable Measures, Inc.

A study released by the Russell Sage Foundation in 1914, based on a survey of industrial conditions in Pittsburgh, was an early precursor to the community indicator efforts of the 1990s.[5] The 1914 work generated a wave of interest in other cities for similar studies, resulting in more than two thousand local surveys on education, recreation, public health, crime, and general social conditions. The information gathered in the surveys was then relayed to the public in the hope of influencing public opinion and mobilizing people to press for reform.

The National Bureau of Economic Research was founded in 1920 and began to amass time series data on the economy. Efforts to improve national statistics accelerated during the 1920s and 1930s. President Hoover established the Research Committee on Social Trends, which, under the directorship of William Ogburn of the University of Chicago, released the sixteen-hundred-page tome *Recent Social Trends* in 1933, covering a variety of demographic, health, and education indicators.[6] The Depression and World War II heightened the importance of macroeconomic indicators. Following the work of Simon Kuznets on national income accounts, a host of measures were developed to produce better data on employment and production levels.

Events in the late 1950s and early 1960s brought about a rethinking of national priorities in the United States.[7] Russian successes in space spurred increased funding for the U.S. space program and new emphasis on scientific research and education. A project sponsored by NASA to study the effects of the space program on society led to publication of *Social Indicators* in 1966, edited by Raymond Bauer. The researchers found that to understand "second-order" effects on social, political, and economic life, a broad set of measures was needed. They did not have the resources to complete the comprehensive data gathering, but the report proved popular and coined the term *social indicators* as a parallel to *economic indicators,* which was by then well established.

The Social Indicators Movement

In the 1960s, increasing public concern over such domestic issues as poverty, race, unemployment, and housing spurred interest in quantitative measures as a way to better understand and solve social problems.[8] The momentum for developing a system of national social accounting was fueled in part by the economic policy making of the Kennedy administration. Using indicators and models, economists had recommended a tax cut to revive the economy. President Kennedy took their advice and the economy responded in the predicted way, with GNP increasing by approximately the estimated amount; this lent a great deal of credibility to use of indicators in policy formation.

Social policy advocates pushed for a similar system of social measures. Walter Mondale and others were instrumental in gaining Senate approval for a national-level social reporting system to institutionalize social indicators as a guide for policy, but the House never passed the measure. Critics argued that social indicators were not so useful as economic indicators because social theory was not so well-developed as economic theory and social objectives were fuzzier than economic ones were.[9] However, public and professional interest in comprehensive social indicators did not wane, and a series of publications in the late 1960s encouraged intellectual development in the field. The publication *Toward a Social Report,* issued by the Department of Health and Welfare on the last day of the Johnson administration in 1969, further increased public and professional interest in social indicators.

Work on social indicators flourished during the early 1970s. The journal *Social Indicators Research* was founded in 1974, and thousands of books and articles on the topic were published.[10] A self-described social indicators movement was born, and substantial institutional, conceptual, and methodological advances in the field were made.[11]

Work on urban indicators also peaked during this time period. Citizens and local leaders sought data that reflected the state of affairs in their immediate environment. International, national, and state indicators have an important bearing on local conditions, but the aggregate level of the data limits their usefulness for making decisions at the local level.[12] Carley asserts that "social indicators have found some of their most extensive practical (and impractical) applications in the field of urban analysis—the study of the nature and the workings of cities."[13] He identifies three main areas where indicators have been applied to the urban environment: intraurban (examining geographical divisions and population subgroups within a city), interurban (measures to compare and contrast cities), and performance delivery (of urban services).

Several large studies were undertaken to test social indicators and to study and compare the quality of life in cities and localities across the country.[14] Government agencies, private research organizations, and academic institutions experimented with economic and social indicators at the local level,[15] which took the form of profiles, need assessments, state-of-the-city report cards, citizen surveys, and socioeconomic data. A review by the Urban Institute of indicator projects during the period 1970 to 1977 identified fifty-eight intracity reports.[16] Interest in urban indicators was also strong internationally, at least through that decade. In 1978, the Organisation for Economic Cooperation and Development (OECD) published a report, "Urban Environmental Indicators," which became a widely used reference for measuring housing and environmental conditions in urban areas.[17]

However, national and international interest in social indicators began a rather quick decline toward the end of the 1970s as economic conditions worsened, particularly in the United States. The impact of social indicators on policy making, never as strong as that of economic indicators, became minimal and the academic literature dwindled. The Center for Coordination of Research on Social Indicators in Washington, D.C., closed down for lack of funding. Cobb and Rixford state that by the 1980s the social indicators movement in the United States was effectively over.[18] It was not until April 1995 that OECD held its International Conference on Indicators for Urban Policies, the first opportunity since publication of its 1978 report for observers to gather and "take stock and consider what developments had occurred since the 1970s."[19]

Environmental Indicators

The social indicators movement expanded the range of quality-of-life indicators beyond the traditional economic ones.[20] Growing concerns over the state of the environment led to creation of a new set of indicators in the 1980s. A great deal of literature appeared in the 1970s and 1980s that critically appraised the consequences of population growth and the environmental limitations of prevalent patterns of economic growth. The concept of gross domestic product (GDP) was criticized because it included economic activity related to environmental damage and poor health conditions and did not take into account negative effects on natural and human capital. It was argued that the productive capacities of the economy also depended on these forms of capital and that therefore net capital accumulation figures should reflect measures of them as well.[21] As a result, a variety of efforts were undertaken to "green" the national accounts and to develop new measures of well-being that include social and environmental concerns.

In the United States, the Council on Environmental Quality published *Environmental Trends* in 1981, and the Environmental Protection Agency developed indicators to monitor and publicize the state of the environment.[22] International policy institutes began issuing publications to document environmental trends, such as the Worldwatch Institute's annual *State of the World* reports and, from the World Resources Institute, the *World Resources* reports. The international development community began to link environmental and development concerns. OECD started developing environmental indicators in the late 1970s and stepped up efforts in the 1980s. In 1992, OECD initiated a program of conducting country environmental performance reviews to help nations improve their environmental performance. The program continues today.[23]

Sustainability Indicators

The United Nations Brundtland Report (1987) ushered in the idea of sustainable development, and the subsequent Rio Summit in 1992 introduced a framework for developing indicators of sustainability. Pioneering work on environmental indicators in Canada and the Netherlands led to development of the "pressure-state-response" model by OECD.[24] This model is a framework for analyzing indicators in terms of the factors affecting sustainability (pressures), the resulting environmental conditions (states), and remedial actions (responses). The UN Commission on Sustainable Development (UNCSD) developed a similar classification system of "driving force–state–response." Both the OECD and the UNCSD developed lists, or "menus," of several hundred indicators for users to select from according to their needs, with the idea that not every country would desire the same indicators.[25] Other organizations such as the World Bank and the European Union also worked to develop sustainability indicators.

In the United States, the President's Council on Sustainable Development recommended in 1996 that the federal government, in collaboration with the private sector and nongovernmental organizations, develop national indicators of progress toward sustainable development and regularly report on those indicators to the public. In 1998, the U.S. Interagency Working Group on Sustainable Development Indicators (SDI Group) released its first progress report, describing an organizational framework for sustainable development indicators and an experimental set of forty indicators.[26]

Community Indicators in the 1990s

Many of the community indicator projects that began in the 1980s and early 1990s are grassroots efforts initiated by business leaders, elected officials, nonprofit service providers, educators, church leaders, and concerned citizens. Democratic participation is often emphasized. This bottom-up approach differs from much previous work done with indicators that was top-down; it represents a new perception of the role of indicators and information in the community. These community indicator efforts are not only about providing information for policy makers but also about empowering and engaging citizens to direct the future of their community. This is illustrated in Donnella Meadows's frequently cited quote, which has served as an inspiration for the Sustainable Seattle and Sustainable Calgary programs: "The indicators a society chooses to report to itself about itself are surprisingly powerful. They reflect collective values and inform collective decisions. A nation that keeps a watchful eye on its salmon run or the safety of its streets makes different choices than does a nation that is only paying attention to its GNP. The idea of citizens choosing their own indicators is something new under the sun—something intensely democratic."[27]

Political changes in the 1980s that shifted control of social programs from the national and state levels to local entities fostered local interest in obtaining relevant data to guide decisions. Advances in desktop geographic information systems (GIS) and the Internet have made local data more available than ever before. The capability of GIS to link data to smaller geographic units has also facilitated emergence of neighborhood indicator programs. In the mid-1990s, the Urban Institute launched the National Neighborhood Indicators Project to develop measures of the social, physical, and economic conditions of neighborhoods in cities throughout the United States.[28] The two underlying principles of the project are that the indicators must be formulated in a participatory process that includes residents and experts, and the indicators must be capable of affecting citizen action and public policy making.

Indicators are the common denominator of a variety of contemporary community well-being movements. "Some places call them benchmarks, some call them vital signs. Regardless of the name, indicators are in," declared James Andrews in an article in *Planning* magazine. "States, cities, even tiny hamlets are using a variety of yardsticks to measure their own economic and social health—and to set future goals."[29] More than two hundred communities in the United States alone have initiated indicator projects to date.[30] The earliest and perhaps best-known effort is the Jacksonville (Florida) Community Council Inc.'s Quality of Life Indicators, begun in 1985 (see the article by David Swain in this issue). However, most community indicators have been developed since the mid-1990s. Numerous Websites and other resources have been developed to guide these efforts, including two handbooks: the *Community Indicators Handbook*[31] and the *Guide to Sustainable Community Indicators*.[32]

The recent benchmarking craze of performance measurement in government has also contributed to the popularity of indicators: "Governments that used to pay no attention to their performance now seem obsessed with trying to measure everything in sight."[33] Citizen demands for greater public accountability and a shift toward outcome-oriented measurement have helped fuel this interest. Benchmarking is particularly common at the state level; Murphey notes that at least ten states have created "outcome measurement" or benchmarking programs. Oregon Benchmarks was the first such program and has created a model for many other state- and community-level projects.[34]

Whatever the framework—Sustainable Communities, Healthy Communities, Quality of Life, or Benchmarking—indicators have become an important tool for community well-being and improvement programs. Much of the work of Sustainable Communities and other community well-being initiatives to date has been directed toward developing indicators.[35] A 1998 survey conducted by Redefining Progress of more than one hundred community indicators projects offers a profile of them (Exhibit 1).

Functions of Indicators

Indicators are attractive for a variety of reasons. They are a way to measure progress, engage community members in a dialogue about the future, and change community outcomes.[36] Indicators reflect the status of larger systems. They yield information about past trends and current conditions and can reveal target areas for the community to focus on for policy and budgeting. In this way, they can be used not only to monitor progress but also to help make it happen by shifting attention to particular areas. They also produce a feedback system for decision makers to gauge performance and be accountable.

One of the reasons for the current popularity of community indicators is the desire to replace traditional measures that may be inadequate or

Exhibit 1. Profile of Community Indicators Projects

Approaches Used	Percentage
Quality of life	41
Sustainability	37
Performance evaluation (benchmarking)	12
Healthy communities	10

Geographic Scale	Percentage
City	33
County	25
Regional	24
State	22
Rural and neighborhood	8

Who Initiated	Percentage
Nongovernment organization	49
Government	35
NGO-government partnership	8
University	8

Models	Percentage
Sustainable Seattle	54
Oregon Benchmarks	46
Jacksonville Quality Indicators of Progress	36

Goals	Percentage
Public education	64
Inform policy	61
Evaluate government performance	32

Note: Some figures contain overlap between categories.

Source: Redefining Progress. http://www.rprogress.org (accessed Oct. 28, 2000).

misleading with more meaningful ones.[37] For example, some measures of economic progress (as with number of housing starts or new roads built) do not include negative externalities such as sprawl, traffic, air pollution, or a degraded sense of community. New comprehensive indicators can elicit a more complete assessment. Sustainability indicators in particular are focused on linkage among social, economic, and environmental factors. Community members have "raised new issues and concerns, hence challenging the types of information systems in place to monitor and assess economic, social, and environmental conditions."[38]

Practitioners have discovered that the process of developing indicators yields many benefits as well.[39] It brings people together from many sectors of the community, fosters new alliances and relationships, and creates shared understanding of community problems and goals. Deciding which indicators to include helps to define abstract and complex concepts such as sustainability in ways that have meaning for the community. This can help create a common vision for the future and help define the community's values. Broad-based participation creates connections and synergy for new groups and builds support for shared programs. Once the indicators are developed, they can become a launching point for education efforts in the community.

By helping to bring issues to public attention, use of indicators can raise awareness and affect political outcomes. This can occur through community meetings, strategic distribution of reports, media coverage, or incorporation of indicators into school curricula. The information gathered through using indicators can affect creation or modification of programs and lead to changes in allocation of resources and in planning processes. Ultimately, it is hoped that indicators will track progress toward change or success, as defined by the indicator program (sustainability, health, government performance, and so on).

Lessons Learned from the History of Indicators

Work by Innes and Booher and by Cobb and Rixford summarizes some of what has been learned to date about use of indicators[40] (Exhibit 2). Because indicators are invariably produced with the aim of effecting some change in society, by far the most frequent criticism of them has been their failure to influence policy:[41] "Millions of dollars and much time of many talented people has been wasted on preparing national, state and local indicator reports that remain on the shelf gathering dust."[42] Consequently, much of the literature reflecting on past experience with indicators deals with trying to explain why indicators have "failed" to influence policy and what is necessary to improve their performance.

The Effect and Effectiveness of Indicators

Several authors attribute the disconnect between indicators and policy formation to a misunderstanding of the relationship between information and action.[43] One of Carley's criticisms of many indicator efforts is that they are too broad in scope: "Misguided attempts at comprehensiveness which result in 'information overload' must be dealt with by attention to synthesis and communication. Researchers seldom wish to camouflage critical issues but sometimes do just that by refusing judiciously to select and highlight data critical to the policy issue. If any criticism can be put to social indicator studies from a policy point of view it must be that many have been too broad and vague and have not concentrated on policy-manipulable variables."[44]

The extreme example is general quality-of-life studies, which he describes as "unrelated to any particular policy and too general to satisfy anyone's particular information needs."[45] Thus they are often ignored. Sawicki and Flynn echo this in their conclusions about neighborhood indicators: "It is imperative that the numbers have a specific policy purpose."[46] Judith Innes, who has been studying and writing about the relationship between information and action

Exhibit 2. Lessons Learned from the History of Indicators

Researchers	Lesson
Cobb and Rixford (1998)	• Having a number doesn't necessarily mean that you have a good indicator.
	• Effective indicators require a clear conceptual basis.
	• There's no such thing as a value-free indicator.
	• Comprehensiveness may be the enemy of effectiveness.
	• The symbolic value of an indicator may outweigh its value as a literal measure.
	• Don't conflate indicators with reality.
	• A democratic indicators program requires more than good public participation processes.
	• Measurement does not necessarily induce appropriate action.
	• Better information may lead to better decisions and improved outcomes, but not as easily as it might seem.
	• Challenging prevailing wisdom about what causes a problem is often the first step to fixing it.
	• To take action, look for indicators that reveal causes, not symptoms.
	• You are more likely to move from indicators to outcomes if you have control over resources.
Innes and Booher (1999)	• Indicators do not drive policy.
	• Indicators can be influential under certain conditions.
	• The main influence of indicators is not primarily after they are developed and published, but rather during the course of their development.
	• If an indicator is to be useful, it must be clearly associated with a policy or set of possible actions.
	• Indicators are most influential through a collaborative learning process.
	• It matters how the indicators are produced.
	• For indicators to be used, there must be not just opportunity but a requirement to report and publicly discuss the indicators in conjunction with policy decisions that must be made.
	• Developing an influential indicator takes time.

Sources: Cobb, C. W., and Rixford, C. "Lessons Learned from the History of Social Indicators." San Francisco: Redefining Progress, Nov. 1998; Innes, J. E., and Booher, D. E. "Indicators for Sustainable Communities: A Strategy Building on Complexity Theory and Distributed Intelligence." (Working paper 99–04.) Berkeley: Institute of Urban and Regional Development, University of California, Sept. 1999.

since the 1970s, takes a more extreme view. According to her, the problem with most approaches to indicators is that they focus too much on what is being measured to the neglect of political and institutional considerations. She asserts that indicators have greater influence in the course of design—in framing the terms of policy discourse—than in suggesting answers to policy questions. In her view, the learning and change that take place during the course of developing the indicators and how this leads to new shared meanings and changed discourses are more important than the reports produced on the basis of the information gathered through using the indicators.[47]

Cobb and Rixford, on the other hand, focus more on the content-oriented shortcomings of indicators. They recognize the point Innes makes about the positive effects of the process of indicator development, but they are more sanguine than she is about the informational potential of indicators. Indicators that just point to the existence of a problem have limited utility. What is needed, in their view, is an encompassing social theory that sets a context for understanding how a given problem arose and why it persists. Such a theory would indicate causal relationships, and the indicators would substantiate the validity of the theory. Motivating decision makers or the public to do something is a key part of creating change, but by itself it is insufficient; "providing evidence about which policies may actually work is perhaps the most crucial step to create change."[48]

Cobb also presents a context-oriented explanation for the relative ineffectiveness of many indicator programs. He sees the attempt to avoid ideological conflict as resulting in indicator programs that are ineffectual for guiding inescapably political decisions about policy: "An ideology provides a context for understanding social problems and assigning responsibility for them. It generates questions for research and tells where to begin looking for solutions. More important, an ideology enables advocates to give a coherent account of the meaning of statistics; a meaning that would otherwise remain buried in a pile of numbers."[49] He argues that we should not shy away from ideology but embrace it as an inevitable part of public life. He argues that "contested truths are more reliable than ones reached directly through agreement," and that this is an important part of democracy.[50]

The explanations proffered by these authors and others address components of this complicated issue. All of the factors identified are important. Attention to both the process of how indicators are developed and the kind of information that is gathered is essential. Similarly, a better understanding of the relationship between information and action is needed to enhance the impact of indicators on policy outcomes. Meaningful change requires a focus on all of these elements.

Evaluation of Current Indicator Projects

Innes and Booher[51] and Cobb and Rixford[52] warn that current community indicator projects may be following in the footsteps of past efforts. Given the paucity of information available to date, it is difficult to determine whether these warnings are proving true. However, on the basis of a review of what is available, it seems generally that the current wave of community indicator projects have taken to heart Innes's point about the importance of process. With their emphasis on the value of democratic participation, these projects often incorporate broad-based public involvement and stakeholder involvement processes. Similarly, contemporary projects seem to have adopted Cobb's position about the desirability of articulating an ideological basis. Community indicators are constructed within a framework of sustainability, community health, quality of life, or a similar structure, often with an articulated vision, values, and goals—a clear ideology.

As far as Cobb and Rixford's point about the need for better analysis, the projects have in some cases tried to draw connections between issues and offered interpretation of the data but have perhaps placed less emphasis on theories about cause and effect than Cobb and Rixford would advocate. The intended function of the indicators seems to be more about providing interesting and useful information for citizens who might instigate action on particular issues than identifying specific policy directions for decision makers on the basis of indicator data.

Current indicator projects have also been designed to incorporate an action component. Indicators are frequently part of an overall program that includes education and outreach and strategies for translating indicator data into action. However, the need for better links to action remains a common theme. Besleme, Maser, and Silverstein conducted a study of two quality-of-life projects, *Quality of Life in Jacksonville: Indicators for Progress* and *Quality of Life in the Truckee Meadows*.[53] Their primary conclusion is that these projects are achieving success in terms of gathering and producing high-quality information and building community but further efforts are needed to translate knowledge and commitment into action.

In a recent article on Vermont's experience with presenting community-level data in an "outcomes and indicators" framework, David Murphey, the program manager, cites many barriers to communities making use of the data available,[54] among them suspicion and fear of quantitative data and political concerns about what the data might reveal in particular jurisdictions. In response, the agency has developed a curriculum around using data for community assessment to foster better use of the data. This curriculum is made available for any interested community. So far, feedback from those who have used it is positive. The primary lesson was that merely getting the data out is not the end of the job.

A recent survey of twenty-one community- and citizen-driven quality-of-life and societal indicator projects in Canada analyzed outcomes in two categories: effects on participants and the community, and the use to which the indicators were put.[55] Among the effects the survey noted were increased citizen and community animation; raised awareness of personal, neighborhood, and community values, issues and concerns; enhanced individual and community empowerment to monitor progress, voice opinions, and engage in debate; and improvement in community choices and response to issues. The magnitude of these effects differed across the projects; not all were equally successful in each of the effects.

For the second category, the study noted that there was a difference in how the indicators were used depending on whether the group conducting the project did or did not have control over resource allocation and policy decisions. In projects conducted by groups lacking such control, indicators were more likely to be limited to use as monitoring, information, and advocacy tools. However, these uses could have an impact on decision makers if the project was seen as credible and if its underlying value framework (for example, sustainability) corresponded with the orientation of a decision-making institution. In projects undertaken within structures or institutions that control policy and resources, the range of indicator use was expanded to include direction of policies and programs and monitoring of results for feedback purposes.

These results suggest that contemporary community indicator projects have been more effective as tools of community engagement and education than as a means for directly influencing policy making. This is in line with Innes's observation that previous indicator projects functioned primarily as education devices. That indicators have a more consequential impact on policy making when decision makers are involved in developing them is not surprising and reinforces Innes's emphasis on the need to develop indicators with the involvement of those who will use them. Finally, the observation that project credibility and value congruence affect the impact of indicators on policy making supports the importance of indicator content, generally emphasized by Cobb and Rixford,[56] and the importance of ideology, cited by Cobb.[57]

It is not clear what direction the community indicators movement will take. Interest in indicator development has waxed and waned in the past, and the future may prove no different. If practitioners choose to ignore what we have learned—both from preceding indicator movements and from the present flurry of activity—it is likely that the current level of interest will not be sustained. However, evidence from recent community projects suggests that we are becoming more knowledgeable and sophisticated regarding the strengths and limitations of indicators.

Likewise, it appears that we are taking advantage of new tools, such as GIS, and participatory approaches for developing indicators. These developments all bode well for the future effectiveness of community indicator efforts. However, although indicators can send us signals, help us see the world in new ways, and facilitate both individual and community learning, by themselves they cannot and do not compel action. Without action, community improvement does not occur. The effectiveness of community indicator projects therefore depends not only on how well we have learned our lessons but on whether we have been able to generate the collective will to act upon our new understanding.

Notes

1. Miller, D. H. "Design and Use of Urban Sustainability Indicators in Physical Planning: A View from Cascadia." In D. Miller and G. de Roo (eds.), *Integrating City Planning and Environmental Improvement: Practicable Strategies for Sustainable Urban Development.* Aldershot, England: Ashgate, 1999.

2. Cobb, C. W., and Rixford, C. "Lessons Learned from the History of Social Indicators." Paper published by Redefining Progress (San Francisco, Nov. 1998).

3. Some temperance advocates also attempted to show that alcohol was economically wasteful by calculating the number of acres of grain devoted to alcohol production, much like a modern ecological footprint analysis (Cohen, 1982, cited in Cobb and Rixford, 1998). Ironically, this backfired when the United States Brewers' Association countered that alcohol was economically and socially beneficial, armed with statistics showing that liquor taxes paid for a great deal of the care of the poor. This was an early lesson in how statistics can be manipulated to advocate political causes in either direction.

4. Cobb and Rixford (1998).

5. Cobb and Rixford (1998).

6. Rossi, R. J., and Gilmartin, K. J. *The Handbook of Social Indicators: Sources, Characteristics, and Analysis.* New York and London: Garland STPM Press, 1980.

7. Innes, J. E. *Knowledge and Public Policy: The Search for Meaningful Indicators.* (2nd ed.) New Brunswick, N.J.: Rutgers, Transaction Books, 1990.

8. Rossi and Gilmartin (1980).

9. Cobb and Rixford (1998).

10. Cobb and Rixford (1998).

11. Andrews, F. M. "The Evolution of a Movement." *Journal of Public Policy,* 1989, *9* (4), 429–432.

12. Hoffman, J. "The Roots Index: Exploring Indices as Measures of Local Sustainable Development, New York City: 1990–95." *Social Indicators Research,* 2000, *52,* 95–134.

13. Carley, M. *Social Measurement and Social Indicators: Issues of Policy and Theory.* London: Allen and Unwin, 1981, p. 130.

14. In the early 1970s, a HUD-funded study was undertaken at the Lyndon Johnson School of Public Affairs of the University of Texas at Austin to initiate, test, and evaluate an indicator system in six municipalities. The National Science Foundation invested $5.5 million in grants to support forty indicator projects. The Center for International Studies at Emory University in Atlanta was funded by the Ford Foundation to perform an international study of forty cities in the United States, Canada, and Western Europe, comparing changes in the quality of life over the preceding quarter century and relating them to the pattern of urban populations. The Social/Health Indicators Program of the federal Census Bureau conducted in-depth studies on social well-being in Los Angeles and two rural counties in Mississippi ("Community Indicators: Improving Community Management." Report by the Community Indicators Policy Research Project. Austin: Lyndon B. Johnson School of Public Affairs, University of Texas, 1974).

15. Sawicki, D. S., and Flynn, P. "Neighborhood Indicators: A Review of the Literature and an Assessment of Conceptual and Methodological Issues." *Journal of the American Planning Association,* 1996, *62* (2), 165–183.

16. Sawicki and Flynn (1996).

17. Organisation for Economic Cooperation and Development (OECD). *Better Understanding Our Cities: The Role of Urban Indicators.* Paris: OECD Publications, 1997.

18. Cobb and Rixford (1998).

19. OECD (1997), p. 17.

20. Andrews (1989).

21. Steer, A., and Lutz, E. "Measuring Environmentally Sustainable Development." *Finance and Development,* 1993, *30* (4), 20–23.

22. Cobb and Rixford (1998).

23. Organisation for Economic Cooperation and Development (OECD). *Towards Sustainable Development: Indicators to Measure Progress.* Proceedings of the OECD Rome Conference. Paris: OECD Publications, 2000.

24. Cobb and Rixford (1998); Lombardi, P. L. "Sustainability Indicators in Urban Planning Evaluation: A New Classification System Based on Multimodal Thinking." In N. Lichfield and others (eds.), *Evaluation in Planning: Facing the Challenge of Complexity.* Dordrecht, Netherlands: Kluwer, 1998; and Farrell, A., and Hart, M. "What Does Sustainability Really Mean? The Search for Useful Indicators." *Environment,* 1998, *40* (9), 4–9, 26–31.

25. World Bank. "Expanding the Measure of Wealth: Indicators of Environmentally Sustainable Development." (Environmentally Sustainable Development Studies and Monographs, series no. 17.) Washington, D.C.: International Bank for Reconstruction and Development/World Bank, 1997.

26. U.S. Interagency Working Group on Sustainable Development Indicators. "Sustainable Development in the United States: An Experimental Set of Indicators. A Progress Report Prepared by the U.S. Interagency Working Group on Sustainable Development Indicators." Washington, D.C.: SDI Group, Dec. 1998.

27. Meadows cited in "Indicators of Sustainable Community 1998: A Status Report on Long-Term Cultural, Economic, and Environmental Health for Seattle/King County." Seattle: Sustainable Seattle, 1998, p. 4.

28. Sawicki and Flynn (1996).

29. Andrews, J. H. "Planning Practice: Going by the Numbers." *Planning,* Sept. 1996, p. 14.

30. Redefining Progress (2000).

31. Redefining Progress, Tyler Norris Associates, and Sustainable Seattle (1997).

32. Hart, M. *Guide to Sustainability Indicators.* (2nd ed.) North Andover, Mass.: Hart Environmental Data, 1999.

33. Walters, J. "The Benchmarking Craze." *Governing,* 1994, 7 (7), 33.

34. Murphey, D. A. "Presenting Community-Level Data in an Outcomes and Indicators Framework: Lessons from Vermont's Experience." *Public Administration Review,* 1999, *59* (1), 76–80.

35. Innes, J. E., and Booher, D. E. "Indicators for Sustainable Communities: A Strategy Building on Complexity Theory and Distributed Intelligence." (Working paper 99–04.) Berkeley: Institute of Urban and Regional Development, University of California, Sept. 1999.

36. Redefining Progress (2000).

37. Redefining Progress, Tyler Norris Associates, and Sustainable Seattle (1997).

38. Sawicki and Flynn (1996), p. 167.

39. Redefining Progress, Tyler Norris Associates, and Sustainable Seattle (1997).

40. Innes and Booher (1999); Cobb and Rixford (1998).

41. Sawicki and Flynn (1996); Innes, J. E. "Disappointments and Legacies of Social Indicators." *Journal of Public Policy,* 1989, *9* (4), 429–432; Innes and Booher (1999); Cobb and Rixford (1998).

42. Innes and Booher (1999), p. 6.

43. Carley (1981); Innes (1989); Innes (1990); Innes and Booher (1999); Cobb and Rixford (1998); and Cobb, C. W. "Measurement Tools and the Quality of Life." San Francisco: Redefining Progress, June 2000.

44. Carley (1981), p. 110.

45. Carley (1981), p. 110.

46. Sawicki and Flynn (1996), p. 179.

47. Innes and Booher (1999).

48. Cobb and Rixford (1998), p. 3.

49. Cobb (2000).

50. Cobb (2000), p. 25.

51. Innes and Booher (1999).

52. Cobb and Rixford (1998).

53. Besleme, K., Maser, E., and Silverstein, J. "A Community Indicators Case Study: Addressing the Quality of Life in Two Communities." San Francisco: Redefining Progress, Mar. 1999.

54. Murphey (1999).

55. Legowski, B. "A Sampling of Community- and Citizen-Driven Quality of Life/Societal Indicator Projects." (Background paper, prepared for Canadian Policy Research Networks.) Ottawa, Ontario: Canadian Policy Research Networks. http://www.cprn.org/corp/qolip/files/scc_e.pdf. (Mar. 7, 2000).

56. Cobb and Rixford (1998).

57. Cobb (2000).

Randa Gahin recently completed master's degrees in community and regional planning and environmental studies at the University of Oregon.

Chris Paterson is a senior consultant with Sustainable Measures, in Lemont, Pennsylvania.

Healthy Communities: Beyond Civic Virtue

Ken Jones, Jennifer Colby

A clean environment, sound public health, and a sustainable economy are all essential aspects of a healthy community. In the United States, responsibility for these policy areas has historically been allocated across levels of government. At the federal level, beginning in 1970, strong environmental policies were established through legislation such as the Clean Air Act (1970), the Clean Water Act (1972), and the Safe Drinking Water Act (1974). Starting in 1979, and renewed every ten years, the Healthy People process (Healthy People 2000, Healthy People 2010), sets targets for improving public health outcomes.[1] Going beyond just the United States, the 1992 Earth Summit in Rio de Janeiro, Brazil, focused global attention on the critical importance of sustainable economic development.

By most measures the environment has improved, but it has not reached the level of quality envisioned in the legislation passed twenty to thirty years ago. Similarly, although some aspects of public health are showing significant improvement (smoking rate), others need greater progress (reducing childhood lead exposure and improving access to prenatal care), and some have actually deteriorated (rate of asthma in children and adults). On the economic front, the country's gross domestic product (GDP) has grown steadily, but its genuine progress indicator (GPI)[2] has shown a steady decrease. In terms of multi-pronged sustainability efforts, there are only anecdotal examples of improvement; many fundamental issues remain unaddressed.

It is in this context of mixed results that we consider the numerous healthy community–type activities taking place at the local level, often under no governmental authority. Despite the concern that too many of us are "bowling alone,"[3] the number of ongoing community improvement projects runs into the tens of thousands. The National Association of Counties, the Nature Conservancy's Center for Compatible Economic Development, the Northern Sustainable Communities Network, River Network, Healthy Communities, the

Note: Development of this article was made possible, in part, by a grant from the National Environmental Education and Training Foundation (agreement 2000–07).

Alliance for National Renewal, and the Mountain Association for Community Economic Development are just a few examples of organizations providing valuable technical assistance and support to communities across the country.

The number and scope of community improvement projects is without precedent in our history. The range of activities extends well beyond the traditional efforts of civic service organizations focused on hospitals, fire and police protection, or children's athletics and scholarship. Similarly, the kinds of things being done are more involved than merely hosting a fundraising event and presenting a check to an individual or organization. Project design is growing in sophistication, reflecting the increased complexity of our problems. New projects are set up as partnerships among institutions to promote economic revitalization, river restoration, social justice, and collective efforts for preventing substance abuse and domestic violence. As their benefits are documented, successful projects illustrate the possibilities to other communities and elicit imitation.

Many of the community improvement projects that address health, environment, and economic development are developing solutions that would be difficult to implement by centralized government action. This expansion in activity at the community level is partially the result of previous experience with government programs. In many cases, realization of national or regional policy goals requires a community approach because the results of government-sponsored programs over the last two decades have been inadequate.

The purpose of this article is to clarify the need for even greater community action to accomplish national policy goals. Although community goals are largely consistent with state and national goals, local efforts can be overwhelmed by regional, national, and international trends. Greater coordination between local projects and centralized authorities should improve communication and lead to better integration of responsibilities. To accomplish the goals that local projects identify and national policies require, policy makers need to acknowledge the importance of local action, thereby adding credibility and focus to community projects and maximizing their prospects for success.

Community-Based Environmental Protection

We have spent most of the past ten years working with communities interested in improving environmental conditions. Issues such as water quality, land use, and natural resource depletion have proven difficult to address using the regulatory approaches sponsored through state and federal environmental agencies. Habitat destruction, especially adjacent to human communities, is accelerating and ecological systems suffer as a result.[4] Most urban and suburban rivers are harmed by a combination of sediment and alteration in hydrology and temperature, resulting in a degraded environment for many species of fish. Resources such as open space and water are becoming scarce in our rapidly expanding metropolitan areas; although "limits to growth" remain an arguable assertion,[5] several communities have placed restrictions on growth because of threatened resource shortages.

The current set of environmental problems is distinct from earlier ones addressed by simpler solutions. For those early problems, a few large contributors to environmental damage could be identified and regulations established to decrease their damaging action. Today's problems are more likely to be the result of action taken by a large portion of the public and are not limited to the activity of a few polluters. The solutions are varied and do not fit into the already voluminous sets of regulations on the books because the sources are so numerous and individual.

Dozens of examples of community-based environmental protection exist throughout the country. There is a national need for thousands more. The U.S. Environmental Protection Agency has acknowledged the value of the community-based environmental protection[6] approach in general terms, but this approach has not been integrated into the implementation of laws that the EPA is charged with enforcing. State policy largely mirrors federal policy, and with a few notable exceptions (Oregon, Washington, New Jersey, and Massachusetts watershed programs), there is a similar lack of effective integration of community-based efforts.

Watershed Health as an Example

More than twenty-one thousand bodies of water in the United States do not meet water quality standards, as determined by state or federal standards.[7] This problem of water quality exists despite more than $90 billion spent on wastewater control.[8] The current culprits in water quality degradation are associated with land use, housing development, runoff from highways and farmland, and alteration of stream hydrology caused by greater density of human uses and increased navigation. Federal statutes and court orders require that the states and the EPA develop plans to ensure that all of the twenty-one thousand rivers and lakes meet designated water quality standards. Because each lake and river is different, a one-plan-fits-all approach does not work. The cost for developing these plans is estimated to be up to $69 million annually for the next fifteen years, and the cost for implementing the plans may require as much as $4.3 billion annually.[9]

Despite this dire situation, there is hope. There are more than thirty-six hundred watershed groups in this country,[10] each organized for the purpose of improving the quality of its local rivers and lakes. Very few of these organizations work under the auspices of state or federal environmental agencies, and their actions are generally not dictated by state or federal statute. In most cases, these groups are seeking collaborative, watershed-based approaches to improving water quality. Central to the collaboration is the general observation that improved water quality brings a broad set of benefits to members of the community, including the persons responsible for its degradation.

One story of partial success is the Elizabeth River Project in the Tidewater region of Virginia. In 1992, a handful of concerned citizens began meeting to consider how to improve conditions in the Elizabeth River. This historic, heavily industrialized river had suffered decades of abuse from antiquated industrial and navigation practices. Clean water legislation during the 1970s slowed the continuing degradation but was insufficient to effect restoration. The citizens began a process of analysis, stakeholder involvement, and partnership building to initiate a series of recommendations and actions. Today, the Elizabeth River Project oversees activities costing millions of dollars, and citizens on the waterfront of Norfolk are beginning to shift their focus back to the resource that served as the origin for earlier prosperity.

Unfortunately, most watershed groups do not have the analytic or legal capacity to accomplish the level of improvement that they envision and that federal water quality policy requires. In many cases, the groups organize in spite of, rather than in concert with, environmental agency programs.

The Dilemma for Government and Local Partnership

Many local activists see governmental involvement as a negative force in local conditions. Environmental agencies have the authority to issue permits for certain activities such as land use (through zoning and building permits), water pollution (through discharge permits), and outright destruction of habitat (through construction of roads and schools). Even in cases where government agencies initiate programs for improving local conditions, their role is often not as clearly pro-environment as activists would wish. In contrast, many local businesses and homeowners may perceive government agencies as being too pro-environment. Government agencies must include all stakeholders in public processes, including those that may contribute to environmental degradation such as developers or industrial interests. Local organizations that do not work under government auspices are not required to include the interests of the development community, and many of them choose not to.

Local participation in environmental protection efforts can be frustrating for governmental agencies, too. Oftentimes, the motivation for local participation is to ensure that the needs of the community are met and that the resources from the community are used effectively. However, local projects tend to generate customized solutions that fit local conditions rather than state or federal agency guidelines. Governments want to encourage locally developed and implemented solutions, but requirements for consistency can keep them from making available resources from state or federal programs.

Although it is tempting to suggest that government regulation be overhauled to grant more authority to local projects, significant political forces would resist the diminution in state or federal authority that is likely to be required. The key to enhancing local efforts to improve community conditions is to maintain state or federal government authority while giving local stake-holders the ability to act.

A State-Local Partnership That Works: The Oregon Watershed Councils

A decade ago, Oregon water resource managers recognized the need for a new approach to managing the state's watersheds, one that would integrate the efforts of state agencies and private landowners. A statewide debate among Oregonian stakeholders led to consensus on the 1992 Watershed Management Strategy for Oregon. Legislation passed in 1993 codified the strategy, which was based on forming voluntary local watershed councils—cooperative part-nerships representing a balance of interested and affected persons. Early efforts to implement the approach reflected state managers' and others' concerns about whether local councils could improve watershed management; council efforts were initially supervised by state agencies. Councils were resistant to state direction of their efforts, and by 1995 new legislation provided funding and guidance for establishing watershed councils, emphasizing their voluntary, local nature. Formation of a council became a local government decision.[11]

Local councils in Oregon are playing a significant role in a number of the state's water quality initiatives, notably the Oregon Plan for Salmon and Water-sheds. The plan is a comprehensive program for restoring salmon in coastal river basins; it represents a unifying vision among agencies in Oregon whose activities affect salmon populations or habitat. The governor's 1999 executive order for the plan specifically includes watershed councils and outlines their roles alongside state agency partners and other entities involved in imple-menting the plan. In fact, the plan recognizes watershed councils as "vehicles for getting the work done."[12]

Oregon may be unique in the extent to which it has legitimized the role of voluntary local organizations in achieving state water resource goals. In 1999, the Oregon legislature created the Oregon Watershed Enhancement Board, directing the state to support local councils technically and financially. The board now extends support and networking opportunities to eighty-six active watershed councils. A recent study of watershed councils in the Pacific Northwest states found that the most effective councils were those that were consistently funded and had strong ties with state technical resources.[13] Although most states have acknowledged the need for a more meaningful part-nership in achieving water quality goals, few have made a strong political and fiscal commitment to moving forward.

Community Projects Seeking a Niche

Examples of state-local partnerships yielding creative results are still rare. In some cases, local governments are developing innovative policies of their own to address local needs. Similar to some nongovernmental efforts, municipal governments seek to identify policy issues that can be tackled without state and federal agency participation.

Projects sponsored by the Columbus Department of Health (CDOH) in Ohio show a progression in the scope of local community-based initiatives. In 1993, the CDOH began a project to determine priorities for efforts to improve environmental conditions. This project was driven, in part, by the need to deal with unfunded mandates. The city estimated that it would need to spend more than $1 billion to comply with laws and regulations on the books since 1990. The Priorities '95 project was intended to identify priorities on which to focus limited public resources. After convening a broad representation of stakeholders, the project evolved into identifying desirable activities that nonetheless fell outside the traditional responsibilities of municipal environmental health agencies. To restore and protect area stream corridors, CDOH approached landowners about land purchase or conservation easement, offering agreeable landowners appropriate public recognition. The department also set up a volunteer corps to map and inventory vegetative cover, land use, flora, and fauna for implementation of an assessment and inventory strategic plan.

Following the success of Priorities '95, the CDOH initiated another project in 1999 to address the issue of air quality. Columbus meets the Ambient Air Quality Standards outlined in the federal Clean Air Act, but continuing growth and the possibility of tighter standards suggest that the city may fall out of compliance soon. Proactive planning led to creation of the Community Leadership to Effect Air Emission Reductions (CLEAR) initiative. The idea behind CLEAR is that by identifying the local impact of air pollution, a local-level project could develop solutions that emphasize the benefits of the investment needed. This innovative approach differs from air quality planning in other parts of the country, where projects must adhere to specific guidelines and seek approval for action from state and federal authorities. For CLEAR projects, collaborative strategies are designed within the regulatory and policy framework established by the Clean Air Act, but decision making takes place at the local level. This is a clear test case for tapping the potential of local action to address problems that must be resolved to meet federal air quality standards but that resist regulatory solution.

Environmental Issues Are Not Unique

Our experience working with and reviewing processes for local projects has illustrated repeatedly that although the individual situations and stakeholders in each community are unique, the environmental issues themselves are not. Land use, water quality, and air quality affect each and every community in the world. Recognition of the importance of national policy regarding these topics is important; we need to improve how national policy is implemented at the local and regional levels. Technical assistance, scientific research, and information sharing are all tasks that national agencies are in just the right place to undertake.

Synergy for Community Projects

Many of the policy challenges confronting public health are similar to those we have outlined for environmental protection. Furthermore, there is a substantial overlap in the causes of these two kinds of problem. Several organizations, such as the Pew Environmental Health Trust and Turning Point, have recently been formed to explore the connections between public health and environmental protection. Although much is known about how the problems are interrelated, the pathways to developing synergistic solutions remain elusive.

Recent developments in Vermont present an example of state and local action cutting across public health and environmental policy lines. The state legislature required state agencies to make information and technical assistance available to a local school-based volunteer certification program and information-sharing network addressing environmental health. Information on nontoxic and least-toxic materials, integrated pest management practices, and indoor air quality will all be shared through a state-run Website, and training assistance will be furnished to all interested schools. Each school that qualifies for certification will set up an in-school team to develop an environmental health policy and management plan.[14]

Concerned with another set of linkages, the Sustainable Development movement is predicated on the idea that the health of the economy and the health of the environment are interrelated.[15] This movement also regards human health and social justice issues as inextricably linked to both the economy and the environment. Given this posited interconnection, advocates of this perspective counsel communities to pursue policies that simultaneously strengthen all aspects of community health. This holistic approach is also a cornerstone of the Healthy Communities movement.[16]

Unfortunately, the dilemmas that make community-based environmental protection difficult to pursue are compounded when multiple outcomes are sought simultaneously. Individual government agencies have missions derived from statute, none of which address health together with environment together with economic development. Therefore government sponsorship of broadly defined community projects is unavailable. Similarly, philanthropic foundations must seek focused outcomes from community projects, and they rarely have the luxury of sponsoring broadly defined community improvement projects.

Bucking the Trend

Despite institutional hurdles, there are several examples of communities striving for better health, a better environment, and a stronger set of economic conditions.

Morton County, North Dakota. Most watershed projects are concerned mainly with promoting better land use and reducing water resource problems. Morton County's Harmon Lake Recreation Area project, however, incorporates important flood control requirements with an additional component: a nine-mile-long, water-based recreation area. A plan is in place to concentrate and limit urban sprawl for this section of the county, which has experienced the fastest growth. The project is a joint effort between the Water Resource Boards and Soil Conservation Districts of Morton and Oliver Counties; it includes state and federal agency involvement and the active participation of local citizens.[17]

Marion County, Oregon. Marion County has created two broadly inclusive organizations that promote stability and community activism. Since 1994, the county has established thirteen community progress teams, groups of community members who work to support children and families and create a safer community. They serve as conveners around important community issues and opportunities, collaborate with other groups, initiate projects and activities, and act as a catalyst in articulating needs and finding solutions. The other major organization is Today's Choices: Tomorrow's Community. A core staff and volunteers act as impartial facilitators, collaborators, and resource persons for dealing with highly charged community issues, and they promote multiple efforts toward reaching shared outcomes. The organization has sponsored efforts such as an economic summit, a children's voting project, and community discussion of regional growth management.[18]

Racine County, Wisconsin. Spurred by the efforts of a local business leader, Racine County was among the first communities nationwide to espouse the values of a sustainable community. Citizens have mobilized to form Sustainable Racine, a community-led organization that adopted high standards for residents and businesses and sets immediate and far-reaching goals for environmental stewardship, economic development, and social justice. Citizen groups have met on ten areas of concern to create long-range visions and concrete objectives for action. Priority goal areas include excellence in education, regional planning, neighborhood revitalization, and downtown redevelopment.[19]

Buncombe County, North Carolina. An Asheville Chamber of Commerce study on attracting new business and industry led to a series of informal community meetings that resulted in creation of a successful initiative. After completion of the study and publication of a community vision, task forces were formed on issues including education, the environment, jobs and job training, governmental operations, children and youth services, and community diversity. Important partnerships have formed in the health care industry, including a locally organized managed care program and a health care services program for uninsured people.[20]

Addressing the Dual Dilemmas

Although the handful of examples outlined here give us hope that a concerted effort to address multiple community needs is possible, the institutional barriers preventing greater effort need to be addressed. Government agencies must develop explicit policies to support community-based action. The problem of having to ensure universal consistency among individual projects can be addressed by shifting the focus from consistency in process by way of rules and regulations to consistency in outcomes as measured by environmental, health, and economic endpoints. However, the difficulty of maintaining focus as communities work to attain multiple outcomes may never benefit from a magic-bullet solution. There is also a need to improve communication and coordination across the multiple layers of government, local and national non-profits, businesses, developers, and the public. The necessity of addressing national policy issues at the local level is clear, but the trick is in keeping such projects collaborative in operation.

And One Further Dilemma of Multiple-Outcome Projects

Local projects are not often subject to cost-benefit analysis. If they were, it might be difficult to identify projects that make sense on those terms since economic costs are more easily measured than social benefits are. For example, the benefits of local marketing cooperatives and coordinated human service delivery infrastructures range over many categories and are difficult to evaluate and communicate. Efforts to merge public health, environmental protection, and economic development initiatives are subject to similar difficulties, although there is a growing consensus that policies in these three areas, as well as social justice, are best pursued in a joint fashion.

The effort to recycle food waste through composting illustrates the difficulty in measuring complex redesign of local systems. This activity has multiple effects. It reduces the burden on solid waste management facilities and lessens the cost to farmers for fertilizers and soil conditioners. Because such a program requires the conscious effort of restaurant operators and users of household kitchens, it may also raise general awareness regarding resource use. Finally, such a program—necessarily local and encouraging local food production—has many benefits with regard to nutrition, economy, and social cohesion. Yet there are very few food waste composting programs in the country, and the inability to clearly identify the benefits to many sectors is one reason. From the perspective of both government and nonprofit foundations, a project that accomplishes multiple positive endpoints is ideal. But existing accountability mechanisms favor projects with a limited set of benefits because it is easier to quantify and communicate them.

Recommendations to Ensure the Strength of Community Action

If this article has been persuasive in noting the value of multiple-outcome, community-based projects, then it is worthwhile to consider recommendations for enhancing such projects. This list is intended to promote discussion and is probably incomplete.

Focus on Results, but Have a Fair Process. Every community undertakes improvement using its own tools and rules. Evaluation and the ability to revise strategies when success is not occurring at the desired rate are essential. Any shift from government authorities to local responsibility must keep the foundation of fairness that is largely required in government programs.

Celebrate Success at the Local Level. We have accomplished a great deal of success in our society as the result of government, business, neighborhoods, families, schools, the military, and other institutions established for public good. There is not yet consistent recognition of the successes that have occurred and will continue to occur through cooperative efforts. Celebration of success highlights the value of new community projects and strengthens the overall movement toward greater use of local decision making and resources.

Acknowledge the Limits of Centralized Authority, but Quit Bashing Government. Many Americans hold state and federal government in disdain for taking too large a role in their lives. The increased size of government is a direct result of the policy goals that we, as a democratic society, have requested. It may be time to get centralized government away from certain programs, but only if local efforts are ready to step in.

Acknowledge the Capabilities and Limits of Community Action. We live in a global society. Some actions we pursue may contribute to resolving regional, national, and international conditions. However, in some cases community-level action may not be able to overcome global trends. For issues such as climate change, species extinction, and international drug trafficking, the solution may not lie at the community level. Planning where best to expend local efforts and energy requires a balance among needs, interests, and abilities. Each community is unique, but the will to promote change must come from many sources.

Conclusion

For several decades, the National Civic League has reminded us that local action is a key to building strong communities. It is now time to expand that message and promote local action to build strong states and a strong country. A strong nation is more than the sum of strong communities. Increased communication, mobility, and commerce link our communities in a sometimes-tenuous web. Only if each community acts to ensure a healthy environment, a healthy population, and a healthy economy will the web be sufficient to meet our societal goals.

The need for greater action at the local level is changing how community projects are perceived. Civic organizations will continue to play a vital role in communities, but future projects will require moving beyond simply handing over large cardboard checks to the hospital or library. These new projects need critical review from our news media and require difficult decisions regarding taxes and budgets. When community projects receive the same level of criticism and debate that such issues as school budgets and new development decisions do, we will have been successful in using the tool of healthy communities.

Notes

1. *Healthy People 2000: National Health Promotion and Disease Prevention Objectives.* (Publication no. PHS 91-50213.) Washington, D.C.: U.S. Dept. of Health and Human Services, Sept. 1990.
2. "Redefining Progress." (www.rprogress.org/)
3. Putnam, R. D. *Bowling Alone: Collapse and Revival of American Community.* New York: Touchstone Books, 2001.
4. Edge, W. D. Habitat Destruction and Degradation. Department of Fisheries and Wildlife, Oregon State University. (www.orst.edu/instruct/fw251/notebook/habitat.html)
5. Mann, C. C. "How Many Is Too Many?" *Atlantic Monthly,* Feb. 1993, pp. 47–67.
6. *People, Places, and Partnerships: A Progress Report on Community-Based Environmental Protection.* (Document EPA-100-R-97-003.) Washington, D.C.: Environmental Protection Agency, July 1997; *Community-Based Environmental Protection: A Resource Book for Protecting Ecosystems and Communities.* (Document EPA 230-B-96-003.) Washington, D.C.: Environmental Protection Agency, Sept. 1997; *Framework for Community-Based Environmental Protection.* (Document EPA 237-K-99-001.) Washington, D.C.: Environmental Protection Agency, Feb. 1999.
7. "National Picture of Impaired Waters." Washington, D.C.: Environmental Protection Agency. (www.epa.gov/owow/tmdl/states/national.html; updated 8/17/2001)
8. *Progress in Water Quality: An Evaluation of the National Investment in Municipal Wastewater Treatment.* (Document EPA 832-R-00-008.) Washington, D.C. Office of Wastewater Management, Environmental Protection Agency, June 2000.
9. *Estimated Costs of Clean Water Program.* Washington, D.C.: Environmental Protection Agency. (www.epa.gov/)
10. River Network. (www.rivernetwork.org/library/libmov.cfm)
11. Oregon Watershed Enhancement Board. Amendment of ORS 541.388. Approved June 22, 1999. (http://landru.leg.state.or.us:80/orlaws/sess0300.dir/0300ses.html)
12. Oregon Plan for Salmon and Watersheds. (www.oregon-plan.org/)
13. "An Evaluation of Selected Watershed Councils in the Pacific Northwest and Northern California." Eugene, Oreg.: Trout Unlimited, Pacific Rivers Council, 2000.
14. "No. 125. An act relating to toxic materials and indoor air quality in Vermont public schools." H. 92, approved May 17, 2000.
15. "Business Action for Sustainable Development." (www.iccwbo.org/basd/index.asp)
16. "Seven Patterns of a Healthy Community." (www.healthycommunities.org/healthycommunities.html)
17. "Profiles on Sustainability: County Leaders Building Sustainable Communities." Washington, D.C.: National Association of Counties, 1999.
18. "Profiles on Sustainability" (1999).
19. "Profiles on Sustainability" (1999).
20. "Profiles on Sustainability" (1999).

Ken Jones is the executive director of the Green Mountain Institute for Environmental Democracy.

Jennifer Colby is a project coordinator at the Green Mountain Institute for Environmental Democracy.

Citizen Participation and Democracy: Examples in Science and Technology

Jill Chopyak

In West Harlem, New York, students from the local high school are work-ing with researchers from Columbia University's School of Public Health to determine air quality levels and correlate them with the rate of asthma in the neighborhood.

In Central Appalachia, concerned citizens have gathered to examine and develop a report on the economics of coal mining, debunking several myths about coal production and job creation.

In New Hampshire, citizens are coming together to make recommenda-tions about the use and availability of genetically modified food in their community.

These are just a few examples of how individuals are becoming active par-ticipants in their communities. Moving beyond simple volunteerism, many people are beginning to take part in information-gathering and decision-making processes, becoming community leaders by shaping the kind of world they wish to live in. What is most striking about this public participation is that it is occurring in areas that have commonly been left to experts within federal research institutions, universities, and other elite research labs.

Recognizing that we live in an age in which knowledge is power, citizens are no longer delegating the tasks of research and development to scientists in labs, universities, or businesses. They are beginning to take on the challenges of conducting research and influencing technological change within their own communities, working collaboratively to generate the information they need to make choices about the kind of community they wish to leave for their children or grandchildren.

This article discusses how the principles of a "communities movement"—participatory decision making and collaboration—are being used to change long-standing practices in scientific research and technological development. Communities and citizens are becoming active participants in decision-making processes and are helping to shape their neighborhoods, towns, regions, and

NATIONAL CIVIC REVIEW, vol. 90, no. 4, Winter 2001 © Wiley Periodicals, Inc.

nation. Through a series of examples from around the country, this article illustrates how the principles of participatory democracy and civic responsibility are taking hold in new settings and in unique ways.

The Context

The idea that knowledge is power has never been truer than today. With the rise of the Internet, citizens now have access to information that was previously stored in information warehouses, large databases, or library catalogues. By using technologies such as geographic information systems, citizens can analyze the information they gather in new and dynamic ways. This information is being used to tackle a variety of community-based issues, from health services to urban planning and economic development. For example, the Right to Know Network has put toxic release inventory data into a Web-based, publicly accessible database that is searchable by geographic location, chemical, industry, parent company, or offsite waste transfer site.[1] The combined use of data generated by the federal government, geographic mapping software, and the Internet makes it possible for any community in the country to know if an industry is releasing harmful toxins into its neighborhood.

Increased access to new technologies is not the only aspect of how communities are using information as a powerful tool for change. Around the United States, community-based organizations and citizens are working with professional researchers to generate information needed to address a particular problem or to set a vision for their community. Citizens are using the tools of science and technology to create community change, and they are beginning to participate in decision-making processes on highly technical issues that were previously left to experts from universities or federal research laboratories.

The reasons for this new movement are manifold. First, research and development collaborations among government, universities, and business are growing, breaking many of the disciplinary silos that limited the opportunity for nonscientists to understand and participate in the research process. These collaborations are shifting the previously distinct roles of layperson and expert. How knowledge is created and who creates it are ever more complex matters that involve an increasing number of players.[2]

Second, expanded educational opportunities have had a significant impact in moving science and technology out of traditional institutions. More people than ever are educated at a graduate or postgraduate level; highly educated researchers are choosing not to work within universities or federal research institutions. Such experts are not only moving into commercial areas but also working within public interest organizations and nongovernmental research institutions. The "massification of education," and the movement of experts out of traditional research institutions, is creating a more informed and educated citizenry.

Finally, scientists are now being held to greater accountability by a variety of communities (both public and private). Recent issues concerning research ethics and conflict of interest, combined with expert media wars that pit one scientist against another (for example, in climate change arguments), are affecting the relationship between scientists and society at large.[3] The general assumption that scientists work in the interest of the public good—by virtue of their profession—is no longer the norm. All of these factors have combined to force government leaders and policy makers to find new and innovative ways of effectively communicating science and technology issues to the public and, more important, to include citizens in decision-making processes.

Community Participation in Research

Scientists in universities or federal research institutions traditionally have dominated research development and decisions about research priorities. Since the 1950s, national security, economic, and public health concerns have been the primary criteria for policy decisions about research and development funding by federal government agencies. Over the past twenty years, however, this has begun to change, with the inclusion of community interests and citizen partners in the research process.

Community-based research (CBR) is a collaborative partnership between researcher and community. Rather than having an outside researcher come in and do research on a community, CBR is conducted by, or in participation with, the community affected by the problem that the research attempts to address. There are many similar terms for CBR, among them *participatory research, participatory action research,* and *action research.* These terms tend to focus on how the research is used, namely, for action, while community-based research as a term focuses on how the research is done: in collaboration with communities. However, these terms are often used interchangeably among CBR practitioners and are all used here to mean participatory, collaborative research.

The movement toward collaborative, participatory research began in the early 1970s, largely in the international development field. Researchers concerned with the inability of policy makers to ameliorate the social problems confronting countries in Asia and Latin America in particular began to question the reductionist orientation of much of the academic research in the field. Working with oppressed communities, some of them began to collaborate with community members in designing and implementing research projects that were directly relevant to the problems with which individuals were struggling in their daily lives.

This type of research became more prevalent during the 1980s, as those involved in international development grew increasingly frustrated with their inability to solve problems related to community development, education, health, and poverty. Development practitioners began to work closely with researchers and community members using participatory research methods as a means of developing effective solutions to many of the problems they were facing.

In the early 1990s, community-based researchers around the world began to come together to share information and resources to advance this approach. The first World Congress on Action Research was held in 1990; it focused largely on developing a theoretical framework for participatory action research. By 1997, the fourth World Congress on Action Research, held in Colombia, included many nonacademic participants and presentations on local and international CBR projects. Villagers from Kenya, Cameroon, Nepal, Pakistan, Guatemala, and Colombia presented information on a collaborative project with researchers to strengthen community water management. Participants in the Urban University and Neighborhood Network in the United States presented a project based in Ohio in which researchers from seven large Ohio cities, each with its own state university, joined with neighborhood-based organizing and development groups around the issue of technology access. Their research focused on the technological needs of senior citizens, small businesses, and people with disabilities.

Community-based organizations and the public have increasingly challenged universities in the United States to direct their research and public educational resources toward real-life situations in their communities. There are many examples of universities taking up this challenge and involving themselves in their communities, directly and indirectly making such resources available to citizens groups and in the process affecting significant change. The Loka Institute, a nonprofit organization with a mission to democratize research, science, and technology, is the coordinator of the Community Research Network (CRN), a coalition of some two thousand CBR practitioners worldwide. CRN members are working to create such community-university partnerships and are achieving significant change in their communities, while at the same time increasing civic engagement and building community capacity.

Examples from the Field

Environmentors, Baltimore

In Baltimore, the Environmental Health Education Center supports Environmentors, a project that gives inner-city Baltimore high school students hands-on experience in community-driven research. The center, located at the University of Maryland's School of Nursing, engages in research and provides training and education programs on topics related to occupational and environmental health and safety.

Funded through grants from public and private sources, the center has sponsored the Environmentors project since 1998. To date, more than one hundred Baltimore high school students have paired up with adult mentors for an opportunity to explore issues such as water pollution, urban ecology, and energy conservation. Students were matched with environmental scientists, engineers, and researchers who worked with them on community action projects.

In addition to mentoring, Environmentors and the Environmental Health Education Center sponsors paid summer environmental justice internships. In a recent program, a team of five high school student interns conducted research with the Pigtown neighborhood of southwest Baltimore. The interns teamed up with community-based groups and launched an investigation of the community's environmental health problems.

With the help of community groups and a public health nursing student, the interns developed a health assessment survey and conducted door-to-door interviews of Pigtown residents. The survey found that residents see trash, air pollution, vacant houses, and pests as the most serious environmental problems facing the community. The results did not end there, however. The group took the findings to the Southwest Community Council, a neighborhood civic association, and did follow-up work with residents to collectively identify solutions to the identified problems. The resulting actions include plans for clean-up days, enforcement of trash laws, and more trash disposal facilities.[4] The students and residents continue to work on implementing recommendations from the survey.

Policy Research Action Group, Chicago

The digital divide is one of America's most pervasive issues at the start of the twenty-first century. A greater percentage of whites have Internet access from home than African Americans or Hispanics have from any location. Computer skills and job marketability are practically synonymous, leaving those without access to new technologies in low-paying positions with little hope for advancement. This problem is national, exacerbating the isolation of low-income and minority communities in both rural and urban areas. In 1997, the Policy Research Action Group (PRAG), a consortium of five Chicago-based universities and community-based organizations, set out to close the digital divide in Chicago.

To determine an appropriate action to alleviate technological disparities, PRAG established the Community Access to Technology Working Group to research distribution of technological resources at community centers, libraries, and schools. The working group, consisting of community activists, academics, businesspeople, technologists, librarians, and teachers, located community-based organizations, libraries, and schools that offer training or access to computers. The group conducted a general survey concerning the nature and scope of access to technological resources in community centers. The study found that youths have the greatest degree of public accessibility, with the least variation in software and little after-school use. Adults could access computers through only seven of the eighty libraries in the Chicago area. Computer centers at community organizations offer adults the best opportunity to develop computer skills, but the survey found that these centers were few in number and severely underfunded.

There are four Community Technology Centers (CTCs) in Chicago, providing Internet access to low-income adults and children. Since they focus on and direct their programs toward community needs, the CTCs are the most appropriate organization for advancing the computer skills of community residents. The top financial concern of these organizations is the cost of Internet access, which in some cases is as high as the rate paid by businesses. Although CTCs have little problem receiving donated and recycled computers, only schools, libraries, and hospitals are eligible for discounted Internet rates. Funded largely through private foundations and some public monies, CTCs are struggling to develop the resources that are available to many libraries and schools.

On the basis of their research results, PRAG made several specific recommendations, among them increasing the funding available to community organizations through universal access and Welfare-to-Work funding opportunities; increasing the number of high school technology centers open to community members after school; and offering technology curriculum workshops that assist community members in pursuing job advancement.[5]

Public Participation in Decision Making

As citizens participate in generating information to help create positive community change, they are also increasingly involved in decision-making processes at the local, regional, and national levels. Stakeholder decision-making processes have taken hold over the past twenty years as an effective way of creating a win-win situation on a controversial issue. Many stakeholder processes have been conducted around environmental or natural resources management issues. These processes convene stakeholders to discuss a particular issue and develop a shared set of solutions or action plans. Although several examples of stakeholder processes have resulted in significant change, in general such projects tend to bring together "the usual suspects," affiliated with established organizations or institutions.

In an effort to expand the stakeholder process to include lay citizens in the decision-making process, several institutions have developed models that bring together average citizens to learn about, discuss, debate, and make specific policy recommendations. A leading institution in the United States is the Jefferson Center, a nonprofit organization in Minnesota that makes tools available for decision makers to better understand what citizens want to do about key issues. Using models such as public hearings or feedback panels, the center is a forum for citizens to participate in decision-making processes on a variety of issues.

In the realm of science and technology, a similar process has been developed by the Danish Board of Technology (DBT), a parliamentary-based institution in Denmark with a mandate to assess the effects of technology on people, society, and the environment. The DBT has developed a consensus conference process that gives citizens the opportunity to learn about and assess the potential impact of a particular technology.

This process has been adapted worldwide, focusing on issues such as transportation, human cloning, fishing, and telecommuting. The Loka Institute convened the first U.S.-adapted consensus conference, or Citizen's Panel, in 1997, titled Telecommunications and the Future of Democracy. Currently, the University of New Hampshire's Office of Sustainability Programs is planning a citizens' panel on the topic of genetically modified foods. The Just Food panel will convene in the latter part of 2001 and the project will continue into 2002.[6] The Loka Institute continues to promote and archive the process through its Website and other activities.[7]

The process of conducting a citizens' panel takes place over a series of weekends. It begins by bringing together a randomly selected group of citizens; over two weekends, a group (of twelve to fifteen individuals) is given background material about a particular issue from a variety of sources. Over the third weekend, the lay panel gets to hear from a panel of experts representing a variety of perspectives. The citizens' panel then has the opportunity to question the experts, after which it convenes in a closed-door meeting to develop a set of policy recommendations about the particular issue being grappled with. At the end of the third weekend, the lay panel presents its recommendations at a press conference; they are distributed to a variety of policy leaders and other decision makers.

These panels demonstrate that lay citizens can participate in highly complex scientific and technological decisions. In fact, many of the recommendations developed by the panels are similar to those developed by scientific experts. Because of its broad representation of society, the citizens' panel is often seen by the public to have less professional bias than an expert panel and thus to better represent citizen interests. Furthermore, the citizen panel process brings individuals who have never before participated in the decision-making process into the policy-making realm. At the Loka Institute pilot, one such participant stated, "We're not the kind of people you read about in history books. . . . Here was our first chance to shape our world."[8]

Such participatory decision-making processes bring a citizen perspective into discussion of science and technology issues and have the capacity to reinvigorate an increasingly disenfranchised citizenry.

Implications for a Communities Movement

Over the past decade, community-based initiatives around the country have struggled to bring more citizen participation into decision-making, agenda-setting, or stakeholder-planning processes. For example, at a recent meeting of the Community-Based Collaboratives Consortium,[9] one of the main topics of discussion was inclusion of community partners beyond traditional stakeholder organizations. Many of these initiatives have recognized that to ensure long-term buy-in from community members, those who feel the impact of a particular problem must be involved in developing the solution.

The lessons and practices of CBR and participatory decision making as described here have the power to bridge the gap between community-placed and community-based initiatives. There is also an incredible need in communities for research and information that helps community-based organizations make decisions about project priorities and that assist citizen groups in their advocacy efforts. Communities no longer blindly trust information coming from an outside source.

CBR, citizens' panels, and other participatory decision-making models are all an opportunity to gather information and provide communities with training and capacity building. Many of the individuals participating in these processes may have generally thought of scientific research as something that is only done by "men in white coats." By participating in the research and decision-making processes themselves, these individuals come to understand that science is a tool that can be used for positive social change.

Conclusion

A communities movement is based on the principle of citizens taking action to create change in their communities. The success of such action requires broad citizen participation—beyond the traditional stakeholder organizational involvement seen in previous community development practices.

This article suggests that some of the best ideas can come from unlikely sources. Research priorities in science and technology have traditionally been set in arenas far removed from local communities. Yet, as scientific and technological development increasingly affect our daily lives, citizens are no longer comfortable with leaving such decisions in the hands of experts in universities or federal research institutions. The models and examples described here have the power not only to generate much needed community-based information but also to transform community development models around the country and reinvigorate an increasingly apathetic citizenry. Information is power. If students, workers, community activists, and local governments are given the tools to create the information they need to achieve change, they can become full participants at the decision-making table.

Community activists understand that teaching people to fish achieves a more lasting change than simply giving them fish to eat. The power of community-based research and participatory decision-making models is that citizens learn how to fish but also understand why the fish stock in the lake is down, what the current market value of the fish is, and what the environmental impact of their actions is. It gives them the tools for creating long-lasting community change, an important aspect of any communities movement.

Notes

1. Right to Know Network, sponsored by OMB Watch and Center for Public Data Access. http://www.rtknet.org/

2. Gibbons, M., Limoges, C., Nowotny, H., Schwartzman, S., Scott, P., and Trow, M. *The New Production of Knowledge.* London: Sage, 1994.

3. Stauber, J., and Rampton, S. *Trust Us, We're Experts.* New York: Penguin Putnam, 2001.

4. Information developed in interviews with Environmental Health Education Center staff, summer 2000.

5. Pasnick, D. "Inroads to Technology: Evening the Playing Field for the 21st Century." Chicago: Policy Research Action Group, 1999. (http://www.luc.edu/depts/curl/prag/)

6. See http://www.sustainableunh.unh.edu/fas/justfood.html for more information.

7. See http://www.loka.org/pages/panel.htm for more information.

8. Sclove, R. 1997. "Telecommunications and the Future of Democracy." (Loka Alert 4:3.) Amherst, Mass.: Loka Institute, 1997.

9. See http://www.cbcrc.org/ for more information.

Jill Chopyak is the executive director of the Loka Institute in Amherst, Massachusetts.

Sustainable Communities and the Future of Community Movements

Susan F. Boyd

There has been an impressive flowering of community-oriented movements in recent years, of which the Sustainable Community movement is one of the best developed. Although the term itself may not be familiar, many of the concepts of sustainability are. Sustainable communities are analogous to living systems in that all resources—human, environmental, economic, and cultural—are interdependent and draw strength from each other. Support is growing across the country for new planning and governance processes that seek to address environmental, economic, and social issues as an integrative whole. A number of community-building initiatives are being implemented in which participants create a vision of the future to protect and restore the environment, expand economic opportunity, and promote social justice. These processes are inclusive, open, transparent, adaptive, collaborative, and participatory. Win-lose outcomes are being altered to become win-win, and diverse participants collectively and proactively develop long-term visions of the future. The greater the number of constituencies involved and the more voices heard, the greater the opportunity for success, since they all have a stake in the outcome.

Principles of Sustainable Community Development

Although each sustainability initiative self-organizes, many create a set of operating principles to guide their governance and their programs. Some develop locally relevant community indicators to measure performance, identify and communicate progress toward sustainability, and guide public policy. Others introduce collaborative, participatory approaches within their respective disciplines to design outcomes that have multiple benefits. In essence, whether implicitly or explicitly, these efforts have been guided by principles and values that demonstrate a shift to sustainability:

- Employ whole systems processes that integrate equity, environment, and economy as equals
- Support planning and decision making that is community-based, long-term, inclusive, and open, and that fosters full community participation
- Create processes that are interdisciplinary and that involve the community, business, and government sectors
- Develop solutions that yield multiple, complementary outcomes
- Identify, support, and link existing efforts and resources
- Share information and develop open communications systems
- Recognize linkages to the regional, national, and global community

Who Is Involved?

"It takes all of us and it takes forever." This is the philosophy of residents of Chattanooga, Tennessee, where conditions were so bad—environmentally, economically, and socially—in the late 1960s that the community had to come together to address them in an unprecedented way. Chattanooga has become a symbol for what can be achieved when a common vision is collectively developed by diverse members of the community. It continues to be a laboratory for sustainability design, enterprise, and innovation. It is one of many communities around the country in which sustainable community development efforts have had lasting impact.

Participants in many local initiatives have been pioneers with a vision of what was possible and a heartfelt commitment to make something happen. They tend to have broadly similar values and share a worldview that challenges traditional assumptions and recognizes the possibility of a win-win solution. They seek the opportunity to create connections and link efforts with others. In general, these champions of sustainability—community members and leaders in business and government—tend to share their lessons learned and are likely to cross traditional boundaries in their work. Irrespective of their background or field, they tend to bridge disciplines and enjoy working in a multidisciplinary, multigenerational framework.

Opportunities for Collaboration

Many community-building efforts exist in the United States; each is making a contribution to the field as a whole. (The article by Tyler Norris in this issue identifies many of them.) One of the values of letting a thousand flowers bloom, as is now the case with multiple strands of community movements, is the diversity of invention that it encourages and the range of opportunity for involvement. Those committed to making positive change happen in their communities may prefer an approach that reflects the culture of their place. The challenge now is to consider the benefits and drawbacks of aligning some of these efforts to leverage existing resources and enhance future outcomes. Collaboration among other movements increases the number of perspectives on an issue and thus increases the likelihood that creative solutions will be developed. Because styles and strategies are likely to differ among community efforts, working together informally on the efforts discussed here might constitute a proving ground to help decide on the desirability of future collaboration.

Principles. Principle-based organizations flourish in the sustainability field. They often draw on elements of existing documents, such as the Earth Charter, the Ahwahnee Principles, the Hannover Principles, the Natural Step, and many others. The Earth Charter, drafted by more than two hundred organizations and thousands of individuals, contains sixteen principles in four categories: respect and care for the community of life; ecological integrity; social and economic justice; and, democracy, nonviolence, and peace. The Ahwahnee and Hannover Principles were drafted by members of the design community, and the Natural Step was developed by scientists in Sweden. There are numerous other examples and considerable overlap between them. Therefore a body of work exists to help with a new collaborative effort. This might be an opportunity to develop and distill a shared set of principles among the community movements. We are in a transition from one era to the next, with an enormous opportunity for entrepreneurial innovation. Principles create a framework for those in many fields to align their efforts. This first step could be the most important one that the community movements can take.

Language and Communication. Language evolves and changes in every field, and each has its own lexicon and buzzwords. Members of the various community movements could explore development of a common vocabulary and a process to communicate and work together. There is a need for a common lexicon and glossary to align thinking in the community field without detracting from the richness of the differences. Links among a distributed electronic framework and e-zines featuring ongoing efforts might supplement existing communication systems and increase understanding about the benefits of a systemic, integrative approach. Similarly, selected graphics depicting before and after images would illustrate concrete outcomes.

Regional Resource Centers. As our organization works with numerous communities, we repeatedly hear from them that they had no idea others were attempting similar processes, and that they would have benefited from what others had done and experienced. To take one instance, the Sustainable Communities Network, an electronic clearinghouse of resources, tools, and case studies on the Internet (www.sustainable.org), was conceived to meet this need. It is a valuable resource; many others like it exist, but they are not sufficient to meet the growing demand for information. Similarly, training for civic engagement, sustainability facilitation and processes, dialogue, and many other skills are needed to build capacity at the local level that furthers the goals of those involved in many aspects of community work.

Unlike graduate programs in law, medicine, engineering, and other professions, there is no degree in civic engagement. One answer might be collaborative regional resource centers that model sustainability systems and offer such training. A number of people involved in community-based decision making have already begun thinking about creating such centers. These resource centers could house representatives from agencies within a given jurisdiction, thereby increasing cross-fertilization of ideas and encouraging integrative decision making.

Strengthen the Knowledge Base. Showcasing initiatives and explicitly communicating their economic, environmental, and social benefits leverages and galvanizes development of the nascent community movement. Certainly there is demand for information about comparable initiatives, organizations, and tools in geographically defined areas. The Internet makes it possible to informally share initiatives across even greater distances. Community movement practitioners could develop shared criteria for evaluating the sustainability of programs and projects that simultaneously strengthen equity, environmental, and economic goals. These initiatives could be catalogued in a standardized format. In some localities where this has been done, individual organizations are able to better understand how their work relates to others and to determine the synergistic possibility of working together for common goals and effective results. Furthermore, this documentation could inform future funding priorities in the public and private sectors.

Change, Evaluation, and Recognition. Communities are all affected by waves of change. Some changes we can influence; others are beyond our control. The question is whether we help create the future we want or the future we get. Community building is an act of will. Political and civic will and persistence, along with willingness to think imaginatively and boldly, is essential. In any municipality there is typically resistance to change and concern about power and turf issues; there also tends to be a silo mentality that results in a piecemeal approach and discourages whole systems thinking and a cross-sector approach. Incentives systems in all sectors generally reward what one knows more than what one shares. Commitment to what is usually an unpredictable civic engagement dialogue and process is essential, but depending on the place some cultures will find this more or less tolerable than others. Engaging and valuing diverse participation continues to be a challenge for many of these efforts. Sharing early and visible results can build the foundation for future work.

It is also important to develop criteria for evaluating the success of projects and for designing and implementing recognition programs. Collaboration among community movements in this endeavor might be resource-efficient and help attract and retain those engaged in this work. The Joint Center for

Sustainable Communities has a recognition program for municipal efforts. A parallel program among community organizations could be established to honor existing efforts and galvanize others.

Research. Investment in efforts that yield tangible, measurable results in one year is commonplace. Grants that support long-term, interdisciplinary efforts are scarce. There is a well-known story among sustainability advocates that Gregory Bateson used to tell about New College in Oxford, England. After 350 years, the beams in one of the buildings built in the early 1500s were rotting and in need of replacement. The faculty gathered and pondered about what to do. Purchasing new ones would be prohibitively expensive, so they called in the college forester. He said he had been thinking they never would ask; three hundred fifty years previously the architects foresaw such a need and specified that a stand of trees be planted for just such a purpose. That is sustainability thinking.

Effective programs require building trust, respect, and a sense of community. Institutions—private foundations, public agencies, and businesses—focus on short-term results. Therefore we need to introduce a common sustainability ethic and metrics that reward a long-term approach, as well as projects that promote individual and collective steps in the right direction.

A collaborative approach with other community movements could create research and documentation supporting the merits of this perspective and thus strengthen the case for this type of anticipatory, preventive investment. A more coordinated effort to educate grant-making institutions about the value of these systemic, interdisciplinary, long-range approaches might help everyone. Presenting the benefits of interdisciplinary programs might also influence how stories are communicated within the media. More coverage of the overarching good news, rather than pieces of the bad news, might constitute compelling journalism some day.

Conclusion

In a recent sustainable community grants program, CONCERN communicated a vision: "Our vision of a local sustainability initiative is one that brings diverse participants together to draw on their collective wisdom to help create a more sustainable community. It engages representatives from nonprofit organizations, the business community, and the government sector to develop innovative and integrative approaches to help build communities that are *environmentally sound, economically vital, and socially just.* The initiative creates systemic change which will have the potential to inspire and inform similar initiatives in communities throughout the United States."

No doubt many of those involved at different levels in the various community movements share this vision. Now is an opportune time to begin to weave these strands to strengthen the fabric of our communities, businesses, and agencies. A principle-based approach could be a shared framework for achieving outcomes and thus engage all the talents of all the participants. The various community movements can benefit from an informal network of communication and cross-fertilization that reinforces, supports, and sustains those committed to this work and begins to move these approaches into the mainstream.

Susan F. Boyd is the executive director of CONCERN, in Washington, D.C.

The New Public Service: Putting Democracy First

Robert B. Denhardt and Janet V. Denhardt

One of the most important developments in political life today is a dramatic change in how public policy is being developed. In the past, government played the predominant role in what has been called the "steering of society."[1] This is not to say that other interests were not involved, but government was the primary actor. To use a sports analogy, the playing field on which the game of public policy formation occurred was prescribed by government and the primary players were elected public officials and policy advisors throughout government agencies. In turn, public administrators, playing on the same field, though often somewhere near the sidelines, were largely concerned with implementing public policies. They were concerned with managing their organizations so that things would get done properly.

But time and circumstances have changed. The game of public policy formulation and implementation is no longer played primarily by those in government. Indeed, it might even be said that now the audience is no longer in the stands but rather is right there on the field, participating in every play. To put this more formally, there has been a reformulation of the steering mechanisms of society. Today many groups and interests are directly involved in developing and implementing public policy.

There are several reasons this has occurred. First, the welfare state has been reconfigured so that government itself is no longer the primary agent in delivering services. Second, the more expansive reach of markets has engendered new means for organizing social functions. Third, technology has made possible greater and greater public access to the policy process. Increasingly, what we call policy networks—composed of businesses, labor unions, nonprofit organizations, interest groups, governmental actors, and ordinary citizens—now constitute the main arena in which public policy is shaped. These policy networks constitute the new playing field for the game of policy development.

Note: This paper was originally prepared for discussion by the Arizona Town Hall.

We are now witnessing the development of many policy networks, each serving its own substantive interests, whether transportation, social welfare, education, or any of several others. Each network focuses on its own policy area and in large measure defines how policies are developed in this area. The result is that one set of rules might define how defense policy is formulated, while another set of rules might define how social welfare policy is designed. But in each arena, major developments in steering society are likely to occur through a difficult and convoluted process of bargaining and negotiation within that particular policy network.

Under these circumstances, the role of government is changing. As we observe the fragmentation of policy responsibility in society, it is apparent that the traditional mechanisms of governmental control are no longer workable—or even appropriate. Traditional hierarchical government is giving way to growing decentralization of policy interests. Control is giving way to interaction and involvement.

This shift from direction to coordination is apparent in each of three major responsibilities of government. At the meta level, government is responsible for establishing broad principles of governance and the overall legal and political rules that frame public activity. This function now increasingly extends to ratifying, codifying, and legitimizing the decisions that arise from within policy networks. Second, government acts to resolve resource distribution and dependency issues in numerous areas of society. As economic interests contend between sectors or policy networks, government is playing a greater role in balancing, negotiating, and facilitating relationships across network boundaries (often through the use of incentives rather than directives) and ensuring that one sector doesn't come to dominate others. Finally, government is also responsible for ensuring that democratic processes are upheld, and that ultimately the public interest is served. It is increasingly necessary for government to monitor the interplay of networks to ensure that principles of democracy and social equity are maintained within specific networks and in the relationships between and among them.

Just as the process of steering society is changing, so too are the roles and responsibilities of elected and appointed public officials—and they are changing in exactly parallel ways. Not surprisingly, the changes in each of the three roles we have just described—those associated with legal or political standards, with economic or market considerations, and with democratic or social criteria—are reflected in different approaches to understanding the role of government and especially public administration today. These changes are also affecting the standards and expectations for assessing governmental performance.

Each of these governmental responsibilities has a corresponding school of theory and practice that interprets and assesses government performance. The first, associated with legal and political standards, is the most familiar and most easily characterized; it is the traditional or orthodox public policy and public administration perspective. According to this school, public officials design and implement policies that are focused on limited, politically defined objectives. They are bound by the law and by political realities. They are concerned with developing programs through the traditional agencies of government. In turn, administrators staffing the various agencies of government carry out these policies. The question of accountability—of how administrators know that their work is consistent with the wishes of the people—is answered by administrators being accountable to democratically elected political leaders.

The next two approaches have emerged more recently. The second, which has to do with economic and market considerations, is based on a view of political life that sees government as steering society by acting as a catalyst. In this view, government officials achieve policy objectives by creating mechanisms and incentive structures to influence actions by private and nonprofit groups and organizations. The school of theory and practice associated with this approach goes by many names, among them reinventing government and neomanagerialism, but we call it by its most recent and most encompassing name, "new public management." From this perspective, government accountability is ultimately a function of individual self-interest on the part of citizens or "customers," as proponents of this view would have it.

The third school, focusing on government's responsibility to uphold democratic and social criteria, suggests that the public interest is paramount and that it is the result of a dialogue about mutual or overlapping interests. It sees the role of government as brokering interests among citizens and other groups so as to create shared values. This might mean, for example, building a coalition of public, private, and nonprofit agencies to meet mutually agreed-upon needs. The conception of accountability embedded in this approach suggests that public servants must attend to more than just the law; they should include community values, political norms, professional standards, and citizen interests. We call the school of theory and practice associated with this approach the "new public service."

New public management has captured the attention and imagination of many of those in government and public administration around the world, focusing attention on a particular set of ideals and practices, including privatization, performance measurement, and customer service. But the third of these approaches, new public service, is ultimately more deeply rooted in democratic ideals and deserves greater attention.

New Public Management

What is today termed new public management has its roots in practical developments in government worldwide, in the set of ideas generally referred to as reinventing government, and in the public choice perspective in political and economic theory. At the practical level, the fiscal crises of the 1970s and 1980s led to a variety of efforts to produce governments that work better and cost less. The issue was framed largely in economic terms. Consequently, fiscal austerity measures, efforts to improve public productivity, and experiments with alternative service delivery mechanisms (including contracting out and privatization) were all based on economic rationalism and the effort to make better use of economic analysis to find solutions to governmental problems.

These ideas received prominent expression in David Osborne and Ted Gaebler's book *Reinventing Government;*[2] there is an extensive literature on the subject by now. Osborne and Gaebler proposed ten principles through which public entrepreneurs might bring about massive governmental reform, principles that remain at the core of the new public management. Linda Kaboolian notes that the new public management advocates administrative technologies such as customer service, performance-based contracting, competition, market incentives, and deregulation.[3] Correspondingly, this movement emphasizes privatization, performance measurement, strategic planning, and other managerialist approaches. What is important for our purposes is that the new public management has sought management reform in government not only through introduction of new techniques but also through imposition of a new set of values, specifically a set of values largely drawn from the private sector.[4] We examine this normative shift in two areas: counseled reliance on markets as a model for government and emphasis on the entrepreneurial spirit.

Proponents of the new public management argue that market-oriented governmental programs have many advantages over conventional ones and that the free play of market forces maximizes social welfare. Osborne and Gaebler favor creating competition between the public and private sectors and among private firms vying for public contracts, among public agencies (for example, public schools), and among governmental units providing services to internal customers.[5] Whether applied to governmental contracting, choosing schools for one's children, or selecting low-income housing, the recommendation of the new public management is to let the ebb and flow of the market guide not only individual choices but ultimately the direction of society as a whole.

This approach runs contrary to the process of democratic deliberation. In an article in *Public Administration Review*, John Kamensky, one of the most thoughtful architects of America's effort to reinvent government, relates new public management to the tenets of public choice theory, especially the idea that self-interest is the dominant motive for human behavior.[6] He notes that public choice theories tend to reject such concepts as public spirit or public service. These are not ideas we can afford to ignore in a democratic society.

Another important element of the Reinvention movement and the New Public Management is its enthusiasm for what Osborne and Gaebler call entrepreneurial government, which they define as "us[ing] resources in new ways to maximize productivity and effectiveness."[7] But entrepreneurship connotes more than simple resourcefulness. In addition to creativity and innovation, a strong focus on ends rather than means, and a proactive stance toward problems, the idea of entrepreneurship suggests that the individual government agent should act on his or her own self-interest (or that of the agency). This viewpoint gives precedence to the entrepreneurial skills of the single individual over the powers of established institutional processes—or over the slower and more hesitating, but more involving and perhaps more democratic, efforts of groups of citizens.[8]

No one would argue that using resources to maximize productivity and effectiveness is an unworthy goal, but there are some potential liabilities as well. Successful entrepreneurs may be creative and innovative, but they may also take excessive risks or run roughshod over people and principles: "While the public desires creative solutions to public problems and likes savings produced through innovative thinking (and even occasional risk-taking), the notion of accountability is extremely important as well, a model most voters and legislators seem to hold. As a practical matter, in real organizations, entrepreneurial managers pose a difficult and risky problem: they can be innovative and productive, but their single-mindedness, tenacity and willingness to bend the rules make them very difficult to control. They can become 'loose cannons.'"[9] As a theoretical concern, the notion of public managers acting purely as if the public's money were their own—that is, being motivated by strict self-interest—flies in the face of a long and important tradition of accountability and responsiveness in democratic public administration. Most important, it denies the public a role in determining the expenditure of public funds and the design of public programs. A far better recommendation would be to treat the public's money as if it were the public's money.

Ideas such as customer service, performance measurement, and privatization have become prominent in government. But this development raises important questions for public officials and for the public, especially as it draws not only on business techniques but on business values as well. Although some techniques have proven helpful, too extensive a translation of business values into the public sector raises substantial and troubling questions that public officials should consider with great care.

New Public Service

There is a third approach and set of standards by which we might assess administrative performance in a changing world, what we call the new public service. Writing in *Democracy's Discontents*, Michael Sandel traces two traditions in democratic political life.[10] The first, which Sandel says has largely prevailed in recent history, describes the relationship between state and citizen in terms of procedures and rights. In this view, government fulfills its responsibility to citizens by assuring them that procedures are in place to guarantee government operates according to democratic principles—through voting, representation, due process, and other devices—and that the rights of individuals, such as the right of free speech or the right to privacy, are protected. In this view, the citizen's role is to develop the capacity to choose those pursuits that are consistent with his or her interest and to respect the rights of others to do the same thing. This view is based on a philosophy of self-interest and holds that government presents an arena in which self-interest can be played out and adjudicated. Obviously, this perspective is consistent with public choice economics and the new public management.

The alternative view of democratic citizenship that Sandel identifies sees the individual as playing a more active role in self-government. Citizens have a responsibility beyond self-interest that extends to an encompassing notion of the public good. Such an interpretation of democratic citizenship asks much more of the individual. Among other things, it requires, as Sandel puts it, "a knowledge of public affairs and also a sense of belonging, a concern for the whole, a moral bond with the community whose fate is at stake."[11]

A central tenet of this perspective is that citizens as citizens share a common undertaking. This collective enterprise, which is often called the public interest, is more than simply the aggregation of private interests, or even the juxtaposition of "enlightened" self-interests. This ideal moves well beyond a politics based on the self-interest of the individual: "In fact, it has little to do with our private interests, since it concerns the world that lies beyond the self, that was there before our birth and that will be there after our death, and that finds its embodiment in activities and institutions with their own intrinsic purposes which may be often at odds with our short-term and private interests."[12] In this political tradition, it is only as citizens act with reference to the public interest—the broader interest of the community—that they can move from a lonely, isolated existence to one of virtue and fulfillment. The process of contributing to the community is what ultimately makes one whole.[13] This perspective most clearly undergirds the new public service.

A number of theorists and practitioners in political science and public administration have picked up on this theme. Many have focused on civic engagement and explored the variety of ways in which public organizations might create space for dialogue and deliberation involving elected officials, bureaucrats, and citizens.[14] Cheryl King and Camilla Stivers conclude their edited volume *Government Is Us* by suggesting several changes that public administrators could make to help bring a new focus on citizens and citizenship.[15] First, in contrast to the traditional administrative "habit of mind," they suggest that administrators see citizens as citizens (rather than merely as voters, clients, or customers), that they share authority and reduce control, and that they trust in the efficacy of collaboration. Second, in contrast to managerialist calls for greater efficiency, they seek greater responsiveness and a corresponding increase in trust on the part of citizens through active investment in citizen involvement on the part of governments and administrators.[16]

One especially interesting treatment of these issues comes from the policy literature, which is generally biased toward issues of market, public choice, and self-interest. In a recent book, Peter deLeon suggests that the policy sciences have strayed from their original intent of supporting democratic processes and may have in fact contributed to a decline in democracy.[17]

DeLeon suggests a "participatory policy analysis" that would engage analysts and citizens in a mutual quest for solutions to important public problems. Such an approach might permit development of a more democratic model of the policy sciences. The pivotal questions facing the policy sciences, according to deLeon, are "empty without a democratic vision,"[18] a lesson of great importance as we consider new mechanisms for steering society.

In the real world, a number of important experiments in citizen engagement have occurred. One of the most widely cited is the Citizens First! program in Orange County, Florida.[19] The project aims to improve relations between citizens and their government. On the one hand, people acting as citizens must assume personal responsibility for what happens in their neighborhood and their community. On the other hand, those in government must be willing to listen and put the needs and values of citizens first.

The idea of Citizens First! starts with a distinction between customers and citizens. When people act as customers, they tend to take one approach; when they act as citizens, they take another. Basically, customers focus on their own limited desires and wishes and how to expeditiously satisfy them. Citizens, by contrast, focus on the common good and the long-term consequences to the community. The idea of Citizens First! is to encourage more people to fulfill their responsibility as citizens and for government to be especially sensitive to the voices of those citizens—not merely through election but through all aspects of designing and implementing public policy.

This distinction between citizens and consumers is important. Despite the arguments made by proponents of new public management, the idea of regarding citizens as consumers of government services is not persuasive. In some ways, it just doesn't fit. Certainly the customers of government are much harder to define than the customers of a local hamburger stand. In fact, it is often because the interests of various customers are in opposition that government is called upon to act in the first place. Of course, there are also some instances in which customers of government simply don't want the service government provides (such as traffic citations).

Most important, in the private sector those customers with the most money and influence are accorded special treatment by the market. Such an approach would be ludicrous as public policy. Henry Mintzberg, the Canadian management theorist, has pointed out the variety of relationships that citizens have to their governments—customer, client, citizen, and subject—and suggests that the label *customer* is particularly confining. "I am not a mere customer of my government, thank you," he writes; "I expect something more than arm's-length trading and something less than the encouragement to consume."[20] As citizens we expect government to act in a way that promotes not only consumption of services (though Mintzberg also asks whether we really want government to be hawking products) but also a set of principles and ideals that are inherent in the public sphere. Citizens cannot be reduced to customers without grave consequences for the notion of democratic citizenship.

We know that people today don't trust government. To the degree that the level of mistrust is due to the perception that government doesn't work well, improvement in efficiency would be beneficial. This is, of course, what the "run government like a business" movement is trying to do: increase trust by increasing efficiency. But it will not be enough. A more fundamental reason people don't trust government is because they don't see government as being responsive, especially in matters of ethics and integrity.

Proponents of the new public service have raised important objections to government adopting the values of business. Practice is one thing. But as we have seen, many contemporary efforts to reform the management of government have gone well beyond adopting the practices of business management. Instead, advocates of the new public management seem to have accepted a variety of business values (self-interest, competition, the market, entrepreneurial spirit).

But what about questions such as participation, deliberation, leadership, responsibility, justice, equity, and so on? In the United States, the bible of the new public management is Osborne and Gaebler's *Reinventing Government*.[21] But if you check its index, you will not find a single one of these terms—not justice, not equity, not participation, not even leadership. And you won't find the terms *citizens* or *citizenship* either. It is peculiar that governmental reform could be discussed so substantially and influentially without there being any suggestion of an active role for citizens or citizenship. To restore the confidence of citizens in government, public institutions must appear to be responsive. The best way to appear to be responsive is to be responsive.

This observation has important implications for the role of government. Traditionally, government has responded to needs by saying, "Yes, we can provide that service" or "No, we can't." It's been called the "vending machine" model of government. You put your money in and hope the right thing comes out—and if it doesn't, you kick the machine a few times. In the future, elected officials and managers need to respond to the ideas of citizens not just by saying yes or no, but also by saying "Let's work together to figure out what we're going to do, and then make it happen." In a world of active citizenship, public officials increasingly play more than a service delivery role; they have a conciliating, mediating, or even adjudicating role. These new roles require new skills—not the old ones of management control, but new skills of brokering, negotiating, and conflict resolution. The key issues for the future of government and public service are responsiveness and integrity.

Conclusion

In a recent article, we outlined the principles of the new public service:

1. The primary role of the public servant is helping citizens articulate and meet their shared interests rather than attempting to control or steer society in new directions.

2. Public administrators must make creating a collective, shared notion of the public interest paramount. The goal is not to find quick solutions driven by individual choices. Rather, it is to create shared interests and shared responsibility.
3. Policies and programs meeting public need can be most effectively and responsibly achieved through collective effort and collaborative processes.
4. The public interest is the result of a dialogue about shared values rather than the aggregation of individual self-interest. Therefore, public servants should not merely respond to the demands of customers but rather focus on building a relationship of trust and collaboration with and among citizens.
5. Public servants must be attentive to more than the market; they must also attend to statutory and constitutional law, community values, political norms, professional standards, and citizen interests.
6. Public organizations and the networks in which they participate are more likely to be successful in the long run if they are operated through a process of collaboration and shared leadership based on respect for all people.
7. The public interest is better advanced by public servants and citizens committed to making a meaningful contribution to society than by entrepreneurial managers acting as if public money were their own.[22]

The need to develop new ways of steering society requires us to consider new standards of assessing administrative performance. In addition to the traditional legal and political standards we associate with the orthodox view of public administration, we must take into account market and economic criteria associated with the new public management and democratic and social criteria associated with the new public service. Our recent collective preoccupation with the new public management has pulled our attention to questions of market and measurement, yet ultimately the most important criterion for assessing administrative performance would be to ask how effectively our work has advanced the public interest. It is important to maintain concern for legal and political standards and economic criteria, but it is imperative that we place at the center of our work a concept of the public service based on and fully integrated with citizen discourse and the public interest. We should put democracy first.

Notes

. 1. Nelissen, N., Bemelmans-Videc, M.-L., Godfroij, A., and de Goede, P. *Renewing Government.* Utrecht, Netherlands: International Books, 1999.

2. Osborne, D., and Gaebler, T. *Reinventing Government.* Reading, Mass.: Addison-Wesley, 1992. See also Osborne, D., with Plastrik, P. *Banishing Bureaucracy.* Reading, Mass.: Addison-Wesley, 1997.

3. Kaboolian, L. "The New Public Management." *Public Administration Review,* 1998, 58(3), 189–193.

4. Terry, L. D. "Administrative Leadership, Neo-Managerialism, and the Public Management Movement." *Public Administration Review,* 1998, *58*(3), 194–200.

5. Osborne and Gaebler (1992).

6. Kamensky, J. "Role of Reinventing Government Movement in Federal Management Reform." *Public Administration Review,* 1996, *56*(3), 247–256.

7. Osborne and Gaebler (1992), p. xix.

8. Terry, L. D. "Why We Should Abandon the Misconceived Quest to Reconcile Public Entrepreneurship with Democracy." *Public Administration Review,* 1993, *53*(4), 393–395.

9. deLeon, L.; and Denhardt, R. B. "The Political Theory of Reinvention." *Public Administration Review,* 2000, *60*(2), p. 92.

10. Sandel, M. *Democracy's Discontents.* Cambridge, Mass.: Belknap Press, 1996.

11. Sandel (1996), pp. 5–6.

12. d'Entreves, M. P. "Hannah Arendt and the Idea of Citizenship." In C. Mouffe (ed.), *Dimensions of Radical Democracy.* London: Verso, 1992.

13. Mansbridge, J. (ed.). *Beyond Self-Interest.* Chicago: University of Chicago Press, 1990.

14. King, C. S., Feltey, K. M., and O'Neill, B. "The Question of Participation: Toward Authentic Public Participation in Public Administration." *Public Administration Review,* 1998, *58*(4), 317–326; Stivers, C. "Citizenship Ethics in Public Administration." In T. Cooper (ed.), *Handbook of Administrative Ethics.* New York: Marcel Dekker, 1994.

15. King, C., and Stivers, C. *Government Is Us: Public Administration in an Anti-Government Era.* Thousand Oaks, Calif.: Sage, 1998.

16. See also Box, R. *Citizen Governance.* Thousand Oaks, Calif.: Sage, 1998; King, Felty, and O'Neill (1998); Thomas, J. C. *Public Participation in Public Decisions.* San Francisco: Jossey-Bass, 1995; Bryson, J., and Crosby, B. *Leadership for the Common Good.* San Francisco: Jossey-Bass, 1992.

17. deLeon, P. *Democracy and the Policy Sciences.* Albany: State University of New York Press, 1997.

18. deLeon (1997), p. 11.

19. Chapin, L. W., and Denhardt, R. B. "Putting Citizens First! in Orange County, Florida." *National Civic Review,* 1995, *84*(3), 210–215; Denhardt, R. B., and Gray, J. E. "Targeting Community Development in Orange County, Florida." *National Civic Review,* 1998, *87*(3), 227–235.

20. Mintzberg, H. "Managing Government, Governing Management." *Harvard Business Review,* 1996, *74*(3), p. 77.

21. Osborne and Gaebler (1992).

22. Denhardt, R. B., and Denhardt, J. V. "The New Public Service: Serving Rather than Steering." *Public Administration Review,* 2000, *60*(6), 249–259.

Robert B. Denhardt is a professor in the School of Public Affairs at Arizona State University.

Janet V. Denhardt is a professor in the School of Public Affairs at Arizona State University.

ORDERING INFORMATION

MAIL ORDERS TO:
Jossey-Bass
989 Market Street
San Francisco, CA 94103-1741

PHONE subscription or single-copy orders toll-free at (888) 378-2537 or at (415) 433-1767 (toll call).

FAX orders toll-free to: (800) 605-2665

SUBSCRIPTIONS cost $55.00 for individuals U.S./Canada/Mexico; $105.00 for U.S. for institutions, agencies, and libraries; $145.00 for Canada institutions; $179.00 for international institutions. Standing orders are accepted. (For subscriptions outside the United States, orders must be prepaid in U.S. dollars by check drawn on a U.S. bank or charged to VISA, MasterCard, American Express, or Discover.)

SINGLE COPIES cost $23.00 plus shipping (see below) when payment accompanies order. Please include appropriate sales tax. Canadian residents, add GST and any local taxes. Billed orders will be charged shipping and handling. No billed shipments to Post Office boxes. (Orders from outside the United States must be prepaid in U.S. dollars drawn on a U.S. bank or charged to VISA, MasterCard, or American Express.)

Prices are subject to change without notice.

SHIPPING (single copies only): $30.00 and under, add $5.50; $30.01 to $50.00, add $6.50; $50.01 to $75.00, add $8.00; $75.01 to $100.00, add $10.00; $100.01 to $150.00, add $12.00. Call for information on overnight delivery or shipments outside the United States.

ALL ORDERS must include either the name of an individual or an official purchase order number. Please submit your orders as follows:
Subscriptions: specify issue (for example, NCR 86:1) you would like subscription to begin with.
Single copies: specify volume and issue number. Available from Volume 86 onward. For earlier issues, see below.

MICROFILM available from University Microfilms, 300 North Zeeb Road, Ann Arbor, MI 48106. Back issues through Volume 85 and bound volumes available from William S. Hein & Co., 1285 Main Street, Buffalo, NY 14209. Full text available in the electronic versions of the Social Sciences Index, H. W. Wilson Co., 950 University Avenue, Bronx, NY 10452, and in CD-ROM from EBSCO Publishing, 83 Pine Street, P.O. Box 2250, Peabody, MA 01960. The full text of individual articles is available via fax modem through Uncover Company, 3801 East Florida Avenue, Suite 200, Denver, CO 80210. For bulk reprints (50 or more), call David Famiano, Jossey-Bass, at (415) 433-1740.

DISCOUNTS FOR QUANTITY ORDERS are available. For information, please write to Jossey-Bass, 989 Market Street, San Francisco, CA 94103-1741.

LIBRARIANS are encouraged to write to Jossey-Bass for a free sample issue.

VISIT THE JOSSEY-BASS HOME PAGE on the World Wide Web at http://www.josseybass.com for an order form or information about other titles of interest.

NATIONAL CIVIC LEAGUE OFFICERS AND DIRECTORS

2001 Officers

Chair, Dorothy Ridings, Council on Foundations, Washington, D.C.
Vice Chairman, David Vidal, The Conference Board, New York
Treasurer, James D. Howard, Century Pacific, Phoenix, Arizona
Secretary, Carrie Thornhill, D.C. Agenda, Washington, D.C.
President, Christopher T. Gates, Denver
Assistant Treasurer, John W. Amberg, Denver

Board of Directors

D. David Altman, The Murray and Agnes Seasongood Good Government
  Foundation, Cincinnati, Ohio
John Claypool, Greater Philadelphia First, Philadelphia
Patricia Edwards, National Center for Community Education, Flint, Michigan
Badi G. Foster, Tufts University, Medford, Massachusetts
Dr. J. Eugene Grigsby III, University of California, Los Angeles
Hubert Guest, Cheverly, Maryland
Dr. John Stuart Hall, Arizona State University, Phoenix
Dr. Lenneal J. Henderson Jr., University of Baltimore, Baltimore, Maryland
Dr. Theodore Hershberg, University of Pennsylvania, Philadelphia
Curtis Johnson, The CitiStates Group, St. Paul, Minnesota
Anna Faith Jones, Boston Foundation, Boston
Dr. David Mathews, Kettering Foundation, Dayton, Ohio
Robert H. Muller, J.P. Morgan Securities, New York
Sylvester Murray, Cleveland State University, Cleveland
Betty Jane Narver, University of Washington, Seattle
Frank J. Quevedo, Southern California Edison, Rosemead, California
Robert Rawson Jr., Jones, Day, Reavis & Pogue, Cleveland
Juan Sepulveda, The Common Enterprise, San Antonio, Texas
Arturo Vargas, NALEO Educational Fund, Los Angeles
Linda Wong, Community Development Technologies Center, Los Angeles

Honorary Life Directors and Former Chairmen

Terrell Blodgett, Austin, Texas
Hon. Bill Bradley, Newark, New Jersey
Hon. Henry Cisneros, Los Angeles
Hon. R. Scott Fosler, Washington, D.C.
Hon. John W. Gardner, Stanford, California
James L. Hetland Jr., Minneapolis, Minnesota
Hon. George Latimer, St. Paul, Minnesota
Hon. William W. Scranton, Scranton, Pennsylvania
Hon. William F. Winter, Jackson, Mississippi

ALL PRICES include shipping and handling (for orders outside the United States, please add $15 for shipping). National Civic League members receive a 10 percent discount. Bulk rates are available. See end of this list for ordering information.

Most Frequently Requested Publications

The Civic Index: A New Approach to Improving Community Life
National Civic League staff, 1993
50 pp., 7 × 10 paper, $7.00

The Community Visioning and Strategic Planning Handbook
National Civic League staff, 1995
53 pp., $23.00

Governance

National Report on Local Campaign Finance Reform
New Politics Program staff, 1998
96 pp., $15.00

Communities and the Voting Rights Act
National Civic League staff, 1996
118 pp., 8.5 × 11 paper, $12.00

Forms of Local Government
National Civic League staff, 1993
15 pp., 5.5 × 8.5 pamphlet, $3.00

Guide for Charter Commissions (Fifth Edition)
National Civic League staff, 1991
46 pp., 6 × 9 paper, $10.00

Handbook for Council Members in Council-Manager Cities (Fifth Edition)
National Civic League staff, 1992
38 pp., 6 × 9 paper, $12.00

Measuring City Hall Performance: Finally, A How-To Guide
Charles K. Bens, 1991
127 pp., 8.5 × 11 monograph, $15.00

Model County Charter (Revised Edition)
National Civic League staff, 1990
53 pp., 5.5 × 8.5 paper, $10.00

Modern Counties: Professional Management—The Non-Charter Route
National Civic League staff, 1993
54 pp., paper, $8.00

Term Limitations for Local Officials: A Citizen's Guide to Constructive Dialogue
Laurie Hirschfeld Zeller, 1992
24 pp., 5.5 × 8.5 pamphlet, $3.00

Using Performance Measurement in Local Government: A Guide to Improving Decisions, Performance, and Accountability
Paul D. Epstein, 1988
225 pp., 6 × 9 paper, $5.00

Model City Charter (Seventh Edition)
National Civic League staff, 1997
110 pp., 5.5 × 8.5 monograph, $14.00

Alliance for National Renewal

ANR Community Resource Manual
National Civic League Staff, 1996
80 pp., 8.5 × 11, $6.00

Taking Action: Building Communities That Strengthen Families
Special section in *Governing Magazine*, 1998
8 pp., 8.5 × 11 (color), $3.00

Communities That Strengthen Families
Insert in *Governing Magazine*, 1997
8 pp., 8.5 × 11 reprint, $3.00

Connecting Government and Neighborhoods
Insert in *Governing Magazine*, 1996
8 pp., 8.5 × 11 reprint, $3.00

The Culture of Renewal
Richard Louv, 1996
45 pp., $8.00

The Kitchen Table
Quarterly newsletter of Alliance for National Renewal, 1999
8 pp., annual subscription (4 issues) $12.00, free to ANR Partners

The Landscape of Civic Renewal
Civic renewal projects and studies from around the country, 1999
185 pp., $12.00

National Renewal
John W. Gardner, 1995
27 pp., 7 × 10, $7.00

San Francisco Civic Scan
Richard Louv, 1996
100 pp., $6.00

1998 Guide to the Alliance for National Renewal
National Civic League staff, 1998
50 pp., 4 × 9, $5.00

Springfield, Missouri: A Nice Community Wrestles with How to Become a Good Community
Alliance for National Renewal staff, 1996
13 pp., $7.00

Toward a Paradigm of Community-Making
   Allan Wallis, 1996
   60 pp., $12.00

The We Decade: Rebirth on Community
   Dallas Morning News, 1995
   39 pp., 8.5 × 14 reprint, $3.00

99 Things You Can Do for Your Community in 1999
   poster (folded), $6.00

Healthy Communities

Healthy Communities Handbook
   National Civic League staff, 1993
   162 pp., 8.5 × 11 monograph, $22.00

All-America City Awards

All-America City Yearbook (1991, 1992, 1993, 1994, 1995, 1996, 1997)
   National Civic League staff
   60 pp., 7 × 10 paper, $4.00 shipping and handling

All-America City Awards Audio Tape Briefing
   Audiotape, $4.00 shipping and handling

Diversity and Regionalism

Governance and Diversity:
Findings from Oakland, 1995
Findings from Fresno, 1995
Findings from Los Angeles, 1994
   National Civic League staff
   7 × 10 paper, $5.00 each

Networks, Trust and Values
   Allan D. Wallis, 1994
   51 pp., 7 × 10 paper, $7.00

Inventing Regionalism
   Allan D. Wallis, 1995
   75 pp., 8.5 × 11 monograph, $19.00

Leadership, Collaboration, and Community Building

Citistates: How Urban America Can Prosper in a Competitive World
   Neal Peirce, Curtis Johnson, and John Stuart Hall, 1993
   359 pp., 6.5 × 9.5, $25.00

Collaborative Leadership
   David D. Chrislip and Carl E. Larson, 1994
   192 pp., 6 × 9.5, $20.00

Good City and the Good Life
   Daniel Kemmis, 1995
   226 pp., 6 × 8.5, $23.00

On Leadership
  John W. Gardner, 1990
  220 pp., 6 × 9.5, $28.00

Politics for People: Finding a Responsible Public Voice
  David Mathews, 1994
  229 pp., 6 × 9.5, $20.00

Public Journalism and Public Life
  David "Buzz" Merritt, 1994
  129 pp., 6 × 9, $30.00

Resolving Municipal Disputes
  David Stiebel, 1992
  2 audiotapes and book, $15.00

Time Present, Time Past
  Bill Bradley, former chairman of the National Civic League, 1996
  450 pp., paper, $13.00

Transforming Politics
  David D. Chrislip, 1995
  12 pp., 7 × 10, $3.00

Revolution of the Heart
  Bill Shore, 1996
  167 pp., 8.5 × 5.75, $8.00

The Web of Life
  Richard Louv, 1996
  258 pp., 7.5 × 5.5, $15.00

Programs for Community Problem Solving

Systems Reform and Local Government: Improving Outcomes for Children, Families, and Neighborhoods
  1998, 47 pp., $12.00

Building Community: Exploring the Role of Social Capital and Local Government
  1998, 31 pp., $12.00

The Transformative Power of Governance: Strengthening Community Capacity to Improve Outcomes for Children, Families, and Neighborhoods
  1998, 33 pp., $12.00

Building the Collaborative Community
  Jointly published by the National Civic League and the National Institute for Dispute Resolution, 1994
  33 pp., $12.00

Negotiated Approaches to Environmental Decision Making in Communities: An Exploration of Lessons Learned
  Jointly published by the National Institute for Dispute Resolution and the Coalition to Improve Management in State and Local Government, 1996
  58 pp., $14.00

Community Problem Solving Case Summaries, Volume III
  1992, 52 pp., $19.00

Facing Racial and Cultural Conflicts: Tools for Rebuilding Community (Second Edition)
  1994, $24.00

Collaborative Transportation Planning Guidelines for Implementing ISTEA and the CAAA
  1993, 87 pp., $14.00

Collaborative Planning Video
  Produced by the American Planning Association, 1995
  6-hr. video and 46 pp. workshop materials, $103.00

Pulling Together: A Land Use and Development Consensus Building Manual
  A joint publication of PCPS and the Urban Land Institute, 1994
  145 pp., $34.00

Solving Community Problems by Consensus
  1990, 20 pp., $14.00

Involving Citizens in Community Decision Making: A Guidebook
  1992, 30 pp., $30.00

NATIONAL CIVIC LEAGUE sales policies: Orders must be paid in advance by check, VISA, or MasterCard. We are unable to process exchanges, returns, credits, or refunds. For orders outside the United States, add $15 for shipping.

TO PLACE AN ORDER:

CALL the National Civic League at (303) 571–4343 or (800) 223–6004, or

MAIL ORDERS TO:
  National Civic League
  1445 Market Street, Suite 300
  Denver, CO 80202–1717, or

E-MAIL the National Civic League at ncl@ncl.org

United States Postal Service

Statement of Ownership, Management, and Circulation

1. Publication Title	2. Publication Number	3. Filing Date
National Civic Review	0 0 2 7 - 9 0 1 3	9/28/01

4. Issue Frequency	5. Number of Issues Published Annually	6. Annual Subscription Price
Quarterly	4	$55 - Individual / $105 - Institutio

7. Complete Mailing Address of Known Office of Publication (Not printed) (Street, city, county, state, and ZIP+4)
989 Market St
San Francisco, CA 94103
(San Francisco County)

Contact Person
Joe Schuman
Telephone
415-782-3232

8. Complete Mailing Address of Headquarters or General Business Office of Publisher (Not printed)

Same as Above

9. Full Names and Complete Mailing Addresses of Publisher, Editor, and Managing Editor (Do not leave blank)

Publisher (Name and complete mailing address)

Jossey-Bass, A Wiley Company
Above address

Editor (Name and complete mailing address)
Robert Loper
National Civic League
1319 F Street NW, Ste 204
Washington, DC 20004

Managing Editor (Name and complete mailing address)

None

10. Owner (Do not leave blank. If the publication is owned by a corporation, give the name and address of the corporation immediately followed by the names and addresses of all stockholders owning or holding 1 percent or more of the total amount of stock. If not owned by a corporation, give the names and addresses of the individual owners. If owned by a partnership or other unincorporated firm, give its name and address as well as those of each individual owner. If the publication is published by a nonprofit organization, give its name and address.)

Full Name	Complete Mailing Address
John Wiley & Sons Inc	605 Third Avenue New York, NY 10158-0012

11. Known Bondholders, Mortgagees, and Other Security Holders Owning or Holding 1 Percent or More of Total Amount of Bonds, Mortgages, or Other Securities. If none, check box. → ☐ None

Full Name	Complete Mailing Address
Same As Above	Same as Above

12. Tax Status (For completion by nonprofit organizations authorized to mail at nonprofit rates) (Check one)
The purpose, function, and nonprofit status of this organization and the exempt status for federal income tax purposes:
☐ Has Not Changed During Preceding 12 Months
☐ Has Changed During Preceding 12 Months (Publisher must submit explanation of change with this statement)

PS Form 3526, October 1999   (See Instructions on Reverse)

---

13. Publication Title	14. Issue Date for Circulation Data Below
National Civic Review	Summer 2001

15.	Extent and Nature of Circulation	Average No. Copies Each Issue During Preceding 12 Months	No. Copies of Single Issue Published Nearest to Filing Date
a.	Total Number of Copies (Net press run)	3,378	5,264
b. Paid and/or Requested Circulation	(1) Paid/Requested Outside-County Mail Subscriptions Stated on Form 3541. (Include advertiser's proof and exchange copies)	2,250	1,907
	(2) Paid In-County Subscriptions Stated on Form 3541 (Include advertiser's proof and exchange copies)	0	0
	(3) Sales Through Dealers and Carriers, Street Vendors, Counter Sales, and Other Non-USPS Paid Distribution	0	1,645
	(4) Other Classes Mailed Through the USPS	0	0
c.	Total Paid and/or Requested Circulation (Sum of 15b. (1), (2),(3),and (4))	2,250	3,552
d. Free Distribution by Mail (Samples, complimentary, and other free)	(1) Outside-County as Stated on Form 3541	0	0
	(2) In-County as Stated on Form 3541	0	0
	(3) Other Classes Mailed Through the USPS	1	1
e.	Free Distribution Outside the Mail (Carriers or other means)	351	217
f.	Total Free Distribution (Sum of 15d. and 15e.)	352	218
g.	Total Distribution (Sum of 15c. and 15f.)	2,602	3770
h.	Copies not Distributed	776	1,494
i.	Total (Sum of 15g. and h.)	3,378	5,264
j.	Percent Paid and/or Requested Circulation (15c. divided by 15g. times 100)	86%	94%

16. Publication of Statement of Ownership
☐ Publication required. Will be printed in the Winter 2001 issue of this publication.   ☐ Publication not required.

17. Signature and Title of Editor, Publisher, Business Manager, or Owner
Susan E. Lewis
Vice President & Publisher - Periodicals

Signature	Date
Susan E. Lewis	9/28/01

I certify that all information furnished on this form is true and complete. I understand that anyone who furnishes false or misleading information on this form or who omits material or information requested on the form may be subject to criminal sanctions (including fines and imprisonment) and/or civil sanctions (including civil penalties).

Instructions to Publishers

1. Complete and file one copy of this form with your postmaster annually on or before October 1. Keep a copy of the completed form for your records.

2. In cases where the stockholder or security holder is a trustee, include in items 10 and 11 the name of the person or corporation for whom the trustee is acting. Also include the names and addresses of individuals who are stockholders who own or hold 1 percent or more of the total amount of bonds, mortgages, or other securities of the publishing corporation. In item 11, if none, check the box. Use blank sheets if more space is required.

3. Be sure to furnish all circulation information called for in item 15. Free circulation must be shown in items 15d, e, and f.

4. Item 15h., Copies not Distributed, must include (1) newsstand copies originally stated on Form 3541, and returned to the publisher, (2) estimated returns from news agents, and (3), copies for office use, leftovers, spoiled, and all other copies not distributed.

5. If the publication had Periodicals authorization as a general or requester publication, this Statement of Ownership, Management, and Circulation must be published; it must be printed in any issue in October or, if the publication is not published during October, the first issue printed after October.

6. In item 16, indicate the date of the issue in which this Statement of Ownership will be published.

7. Item 17 must be signed.

Failure to file or publish a statement of ownership may lead to suspension of Periodicals authorization.

PS Form 3526, October 1999 (Reverse)